Hidden Treasures of Transylvania

The Saxon Fortified Churches

Verborgene Schätze in Siebenbürgen

Die Sächsischen Kirchenburgen

© COPYRIGHT Mioritics Association

BUCHAREST / ROMANIA 2011
e-mail: sibiu@culture-routes.lu
tel.: 0788 301830
All rights reserved

www.culture-routes.ro
www.kirchenburgen.ro
www.fortified-churches.com

CIP description of the National Library of Romania

Hidden treasures of Transylvania : the saxon fortified churches = Verborgene Schätze in Siebenbürgen : die sächsischen Kirchenburgen / Mihai Dragomir (coord.), Ilinca Maican, Christa Richter, ... - Bucharest : Mioritics 2011
ISBN: 978-606-8320-02-1

I. Dragomir, Mihai (coord.)
II. Maican, Ilinca
III. Richter, Christa

726.54(498.4)

Coordinator: MIHAI DRAGOMIR
Cover: ALEXANDRA BARDAN

Layout: ALEXANDRA BARDAN
        DANIEL SECĂRESCU

Ready to be printed: September 2011

Printed in Romania, RH Printing

Hidden Treasures of Transylvania

The Saxon Fortified Churches

Verborgene Schätze in Siebenbürgen

Die sächsischen Kirchenburgen

My Transylvania
Transilvania Mea
Mein Siebenbürgen

Some say that in The Beginning there were giants. They had the face of a human, but they were very, very big and when they wanted to borrow something from their neighbor they traveled hundreds of miles and they were back in no time. One day, a giant girl found something curiously small and strange, took it in the palm and showed it to her mom: "look I found a bug?". But it was neither bug nor warm and her mom said: "go back and put him where you found him, this is a Human and they will inherit the Earth". And so it happened...

And after humans there will be very small creatures, dwarf people, who will climb a flower by ladder and they would enter 12 in an eggshell. They will be God's favorites; because there was a time for giants (physical power), followed by us, humans (the age of mind and reason) and in the end the age of holiness, the age of God.

If one pays attention can still witness today markings of the giants passing, especially giants graves, the small and sudden hills in the middle of a field. There are 3 of this kind right before Apold on the road from Agnita to Sighisoara. You do know now there are giants' graves!

Es heißt, zu Beginn seien Riesen auf der Welt gewesen. Diese waren von menschlichem Aussehen, aber sehr groß, so dass sie, wenn ihnen das Maismehl ausging, hunderte Kilometer bis zum Nachbarn gingen, um von diesem welches zu verlangen. Bis sie zurückkamen, begann das vorher aufgestellte Wasser gerade erst zu kochen. Eines Tages fand ein Riesenmädchen etwas Merkwürdiges, Kleines, das sie auf ihre Handfläche nahm und heimtrug; sie war über dieses merkwürdige Ding höchst verwundert. Sie zeigte es ihrer Mutter: "Schau ein Käferchen, das in der Erde buddelte." Doch es war kein Käfer, und die Mutter sagte: "geh und tue das Ding zurück, denn dies ist ein Mensch, und die Menschen werden die Erde erben". Und so geschah es auch.

Und nach den Menschen werden noch kleinere Wesen auftauchen, die mittels einer Leiter eine Brennessel erklettern, und von denen ein Dutzend in einer Eierschale Platz haben werden. Diese wird Gott am liebsten haben. Nach einer Zeit der physischen Kräfte folgte die Zeit der Gedankenkraft (wir Menschen, nun ja) und schließlich wird es die Zeit der Heiligkeit geben, die Zeit Gottes.

Spuren dieser Zeiten sieht man heute noch, man muss nur genau hinsehen, oder von jemandem darauf aufmerksam gemacht werden. Vor allem Gräber von Riesen, also die Hügel, welche die Archäologen Tumuli nennen. Auf dem Weg zwischen Agneteln (Agnita) und Schäßburg (Sighisoara) gibt es drei davon, knapp vor Trappold (Apold).

FOREWORD

The history of the fortified Saxon churches began in the 12th century, when King Geza II of Hungary assigned more than 2,500 German colonists to protect and develop the southeastern part of Transylvania ("the land beyond the forest"), a fertile plateau surrounded by the Carpathians. A document issued in 1224 by King Andrew II named the "golden letter of freedom," or "Andreaneum," gave the colonists special rights and privileges which ensured their autonomy and significantly influenced the development of their villages.

From the very beginning, the churches played an important role in the life of these new communities, which had a spectacular social and commercial development in a relatively short period of time.

The first Ottoman invasion occurred in 1395 and was followed by nearly a century of devastating attacks by the Turk soldiers.

Local communities had limited resources compared to larger towns and the citizens were desperately looking for defensive solutions to protect their lives and belongings. The Saxons chose the church building as their ultimate refuge from the invasions, 'avant-la-lettre' confirming Luther's words: "God's name is the Shield!"

EINLEITUNG

Die Geschichte der siebenbürgisch-sächsischen Kirchenburgen geht auf das XII. Jahrhundert zurück, als der ungarische König Geza der Zweite über 2500 deutsche Kolonisten einlud, im „Land hinter den Wäldern" (Transsylvanien) zu siedeln, um die wirtschaftliche Entwicklung dieses fruchtbaren Landstrichs am Karpatenbogen voranzutreiben. König Andreas der Zweite erläßt 1224 eine Bulle, den „Andreanischen Freibrief", der ihnen weitreichende Rechte gewährt und die Autonomie des sogenannten „Königsbodens" festschreibt, was viel zum Aufblühen der neuen Ortschaften beiträgt.

Die Kirche war von Anfang an eine der wichtigsten Stützen der neuentstandenen Gemeinden, die in kürzester Zeit eine erstaunliche wirtschaftliche Leistungskraft entwickelten.

1395 findet der erste Türkeneinfall statt. Über ein Jahrhundert lang brandschatzten die Kriegerhorden unter dem Zeichen des Halbmonds die Ortschaften des „Königsbodens".

Als Reaktion darauf versuchen die Dorfgemeinden Abwehrstrategien zu finden. Und die letzte Zuflucht der bedrängten Einwohner wird die Kirche sein, im realen wie im bildlichen Sinne - eine Vorwegnahme von Luthers Worten vom Glauben als fester Burg.

In the church, the Middle Age man felt protected by the Divinity. Through a papal bull issued by Pope Nicholas II, people wanted by the authorities, from tax dodgers to murderers, could be sheltered in churches, while anyone who would use force to enter a church would have been excommunicated. Thus the church was considered a refuge of maximum security.

The church was also the largest and highest building in the village, with room to shelter the entire community. Positioned in the centre of the settlement, it was also easily accessible for all villagers in case of enemy attack.

In the following decades, the churches were refurbished and even partly rebuilt, depending on the economic and financial power of each community, so as to become real fortresses, able to offer even greater protection the villagers during the sieges.

The bell-tower was endowed with shooting positions and wall passages, thus becoming the front line defensive tower. The chorus was elevated and fortified, giving it a defensive role as well, and above the altar, a defensive level was erected which also contained shooting positions.

In the 15th century, precincts with specific defensive roles were built: bastions, different types of towers, ditches and zwingers. Food warehouses were also constructed.

It wasn't until after the last Ottoman invasion of 1788 that the churches regained their unique religious role. Despite the numerous hardships, the Saxons managed to further develop their communities both politically and economically.

Der mittelalterlichen Glaubensvorstellung entsprechend, war das Gotteshaus Ausdruck göttlicher Fügung. Gemäß eines Erlasses Papst Nikolaus' des Zweiten gewährte die Kirche auch Mördern und Schuldnern Asyl, während ihre Häscher, die mit Gewalt in die Kirche eindrangen, der Bannstrahl der Exkommunikation traf. So festigte sich in der mittelalterlichen Vorstellungswelt der Glaube an die Kirche als sicherer Ort.

Rein bautechnisch waren die Kirchen die mächtigsten Gebäuden der Ortschaften, in denen die gesamte Gemeinde untergebracht werden konnte. Meist auf einer Anhöhe in der Mitte der Ortschaft gelegen, waren sie auch zum schnellen Rückzug im Falle eines Angriffs geeignet.

In den Zeitabständen zwischen den Türkeneinfällen erfuhren die Kirchenanlagen bauliche Umgestaltungen, sie wurden zu richtigen Burgen ausgebaut, um den Einwohnern besseren Schutz zu gewähren während einer Belagerung.

Im Kirchturm wurden Schießscharten angebracht und die Brüstung wurde festungsmäßig ausgebaut. Der hohe Kirchenchor erhielt ebenfalls eine Wehrfunktion, während über dem Altar eine zusätzliche Verteidigungshöhe errichtet wurde.

Im 15.Jahrhundert kommen weitere spezifische Elemente der Wehranlagen hinzu: Basteien, Wehrtürme unterschiedlichster Höhe, Gräben und Zwinger. Ebenso werden Lagerräume für Lebensmittel geschaffen, Aufbewahrungsorte im Falle längerer Belagerungen.

Ihren ausschließlich religiösen Diensten vorbehaltenen Charakter erhalten die Kirchen erst 1788, nach der letzten Türkeninvasion, zurück. Doch allen Widrigkeiten der Geschichte zum Trotz, gelang es den Siebenbürger Sachsen mit viel Handwerksgeschick und ungewöhnlichem Gemeinsinn, ein blühendes Wirtschafts- und Sozialleben aufrechtzuerhalten.

"Although since the end of the 18th century the fortified churches lost their defensive role, they were still carefully maintained by the villagers. Aware that their own identity could not have been preserved in the absence of the protection offered by the fortified churches, the local communities unofficially acknowledged the cultural identity value of these buildings," Hanna Derer (2001).

The unfortunate events of World War II shook all of Europe but also marked the beginning of the end of eight hundred years of Saxon history in Transylvania. The war-time deportations were followed by a massive emigration process as a result of the severe living conditions during the communist regime. The fall of Ceausescu's dictatorship in 1989 opened the borders for the last wave of Saxon emigration, mainly to the reunited Germany.

The massive emigrations left behind only a handful of elderly Saxons who tried to take care of the churches and their heritage. Except for some, the vast majority of the fortified churches began to fall into ruin, and an important number of objects of worship fell into the hands of thieves and antique merchants. The elderly villagers tell travellers the story of this dying civilization. The buildings remind one of the past glories, but the few Saxons left behind to take care of them cannot prevent their inevitable decay.

As a sign of recognition to their uniqueness, 7 out of the over 150 Saxon churches are on the UNESCO's World Heritage list. Other organizations are currently trying to restore several sites so as to rescue as many remnants of the Saxon civilization as possible.

So meint Hanna Derer im Jahre 2001, dass die Wehranlagen auch weiterhin im gleichen Maße gepflegt und instande gehalten wurden, obwohl sie ihrer Wehrfunktion verlustig gegangen waren. Die Gemeinden, deren physischen Erhalt sie über die Jahrhunderte gesichert hatten, maßen ihnen nun - wenn auch unausgesprochen die gleiche Wichtigkeit zu bei der Bewahrung der kulturellen Identität.

Die Kriegswirren, die durch den Zweiten Weltkrieg ausgelöst wurden, leiteten das Ende der über acht Jahrhunderte andauernden Geschichte der Siebenbürger Sachsen in der angestammten Form ein. Den Verschleppungen nach Kriegsende folgten massive Auswanderungswellen in den Westen, verursacht vor allem durch die schlechten Lebensverhältnisse während der kommunistischen Herrschaft. Als sich dann 1989, nach dem Fall der Ceausescu Diktatur die Grenzen öffneten, fand der Exodus statt, vor allem ins wiedervereinigte Deutschland.

Am Ende der Auswanderungswellen blieb nur mehr eine Handvoll vor allem älterer Sachsen zurück. Sie versuchen im Rahmen ihrer Kräfte, das Erbe der Ahnen zu bewahren. Doch diese reichen nicht aus, um den Verfall der meisten Kirchenburgen aufzuhalten. Ebensowenig kann - mit einigen Ausnahmen der Kirchenschatz an geweihten Gegenständen und Kulturgütern vor Diebeshand geschützt werden. Die glorreiche Vergangenheit dieser außergewöhnlichen Volksgemeinschaft wurde ins Reich der Erzählungen und Überlieferungen verbannt, die der Besucher mit etwas Glück von einem Dorfalten zu hören kriegen kann.

Die wuchtigen Bauten erinnern an vergangene Pracht, doch die wenigen verbliebenen Siebenbürger Sachsen können kaum gegen ihren Verfall ankämpfen.

Als Anerkennung ihres einmaligen Wertes wurden 7 der über 150 existierenden Kirchburgen auf die Liste des Weltkulturerbes der UNESCO eingetragen. Zur Zeit gibt es mehrere Organisationen, Vereine und Stiftungen, die sich die Bewahrung der siebenbürgisch-sächsischen Kulturdenkmäler zum Ziel gesetzt haben.

The Lard Tower

There is almost no Saxon church in Transylvania which does not have such a tower. At a first glance it is no different from the other towers: defensive purpose, announcing invaders; the works.

But starting every winter and for almost all year long, sometimes until late fall, one of these towers held something special – the lard reserve of the villagers. The smoked pieces of lard were hung on hooks and bore the owners' stamp on their lower end.

This was customary, because keeping everything in one place does not mean it belongs to everyone. Each family had its own storage place inside the tower and a distinctive mark on the pieces of lard they owened. During the year, they would take a piece of their lard, anytime they needed, but usually on Sundays, as the tower may have been closed on week days. The owner would cut as much as he needed and than stamp the lower end of the remaining part.

In this way thefts did not go unnoticed, even if the culprit was silent as a rock, and it appears that this system was enough to prevent lard from being stolen.

Der Speckturm

Es gibt kaum eine sächsische Kirchenburg ohne einen Turm, der auf den ersten Blick zwar nichts Besonderes an sich hat, allerdings früher eine Art gemeinschaftliche Speisekammer voller Speck war! Die geräucherten, meterlangen Speckschwarten hingen an riesigen Haken von den Balken und Wänden. Die Speckseiten selber trugen am unteren Ende, dort wo der Speck stückweise abgetrennt wurde, den Stempel des Besitzers.

Jede Familie im Dorf hatte einen Stammplatz im Speckturm und einen Stempel für die Markierung der Schwarten. Am Sonntag war in der Regel Specktag - der Turm wurde aufgeschlossen und die Besitzer holten sich eine neue Portion von diesem traditionellen Lebensmittel ab, für die nächste Woche. Die frische Schnittstelle wurde abgestempelt - so konnte sich kein anderer von dieser Tafel bedienen. Der potentielle Speckdieb hätte seine Missetat zwar verschweigen können, dennoch hätte sich der Diebstahl herumgesprochen, und allein schon die mögliche Verdächtigung wirkte abschreckend und disziplinierend auf die Mitglieder der Dorfgemeinschaft.

Brașov

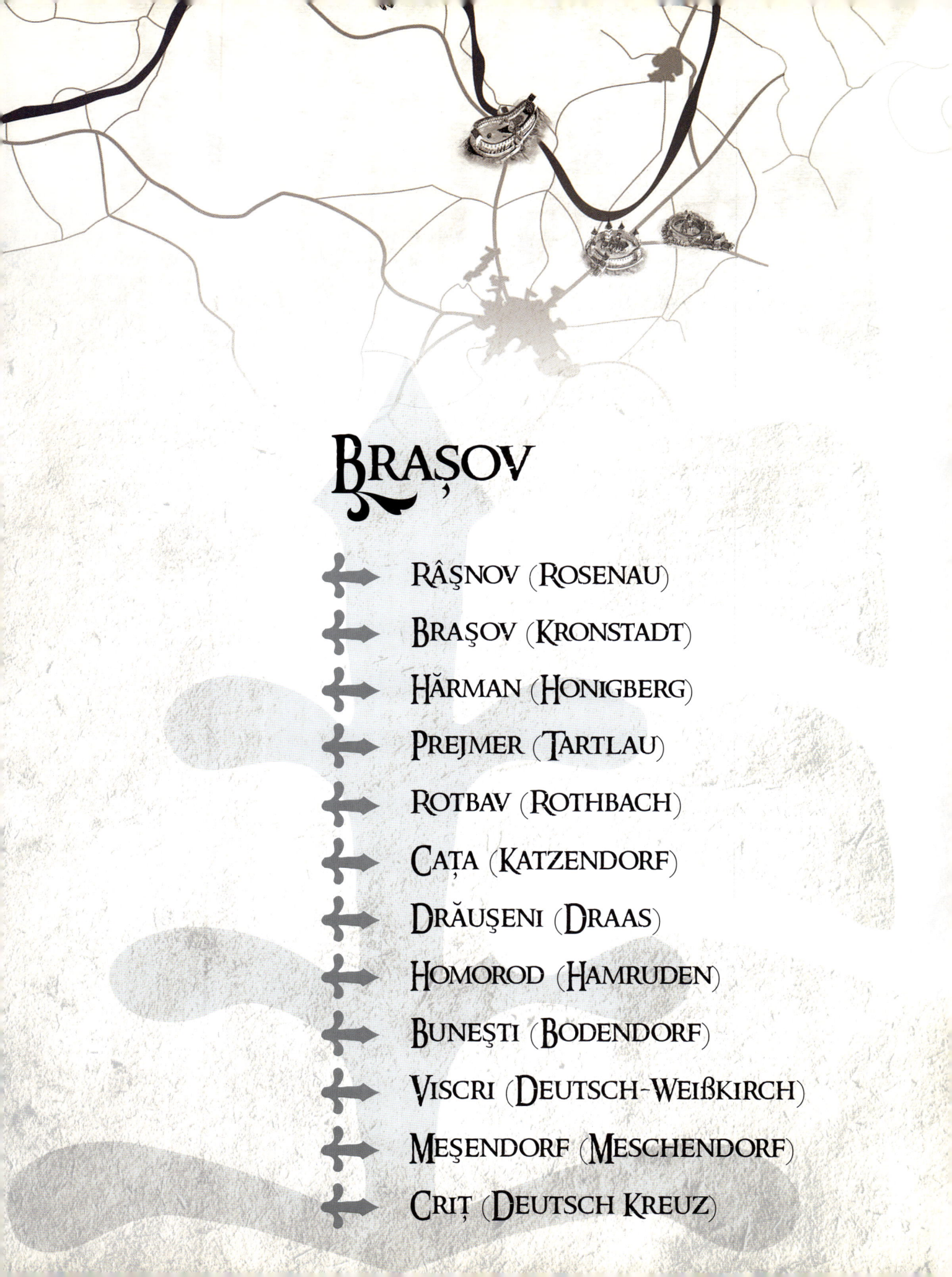

➤ Râșnov (Rosenau)

➤ Brașov (Kronstadt)

➤ Hărman (Honigberg)

➤ Prejmer (Tartlau)

➤ Rotbav (Rothbach)

➤ Cața (Katzendorf)

➤ Drăușeni (Draas)

➤ Homorod (Hamruden)

➤ Bunești (Bodendorf)

➤ Viscri (Deutsch-Weißkirch)

➤ Meșendorf (Meschendorf)

➤ Criț (Deutsch Kreuz)

RÂŞNOV
ROSENAU

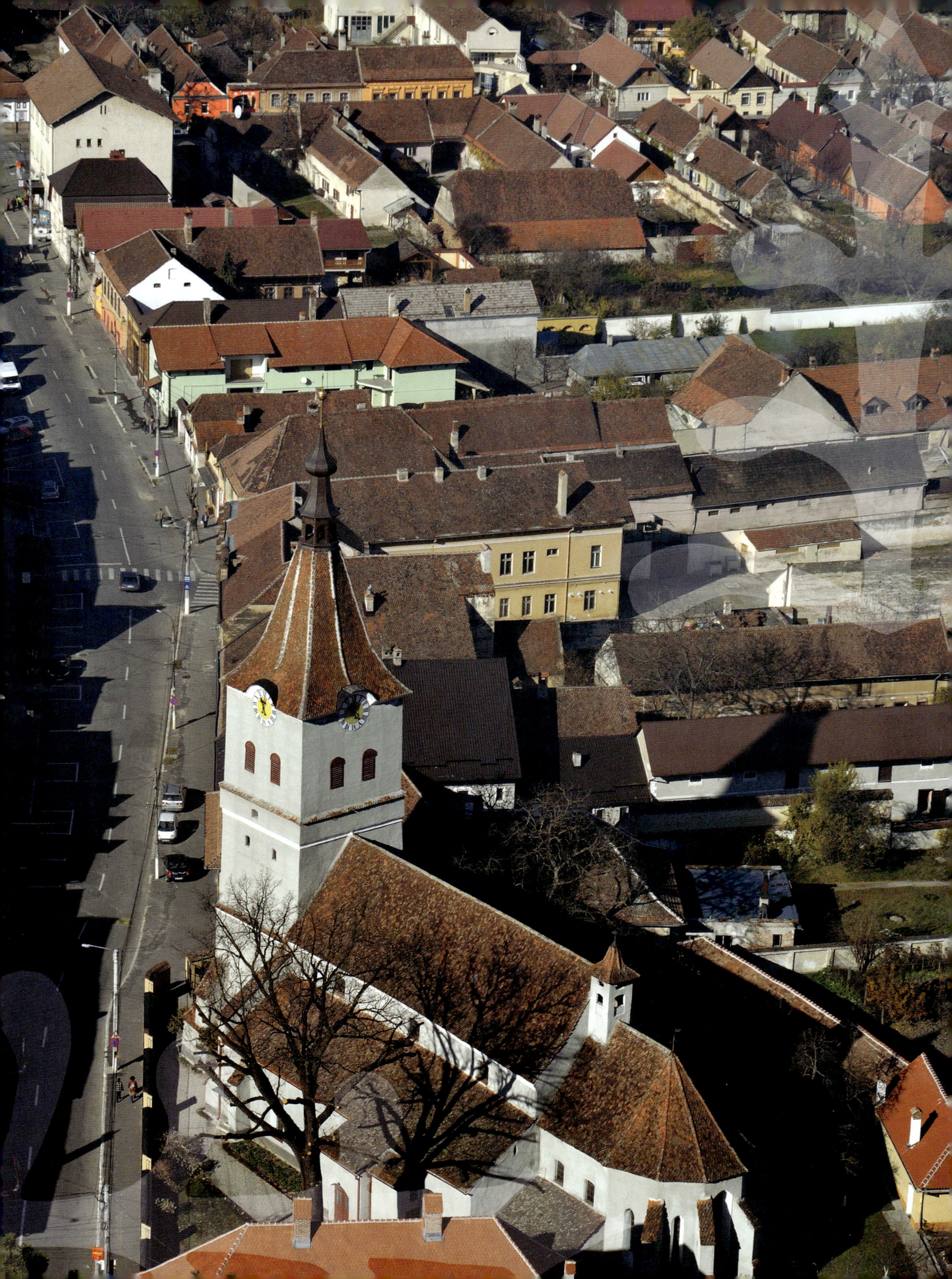

BRAȘOV
KRONSTADT

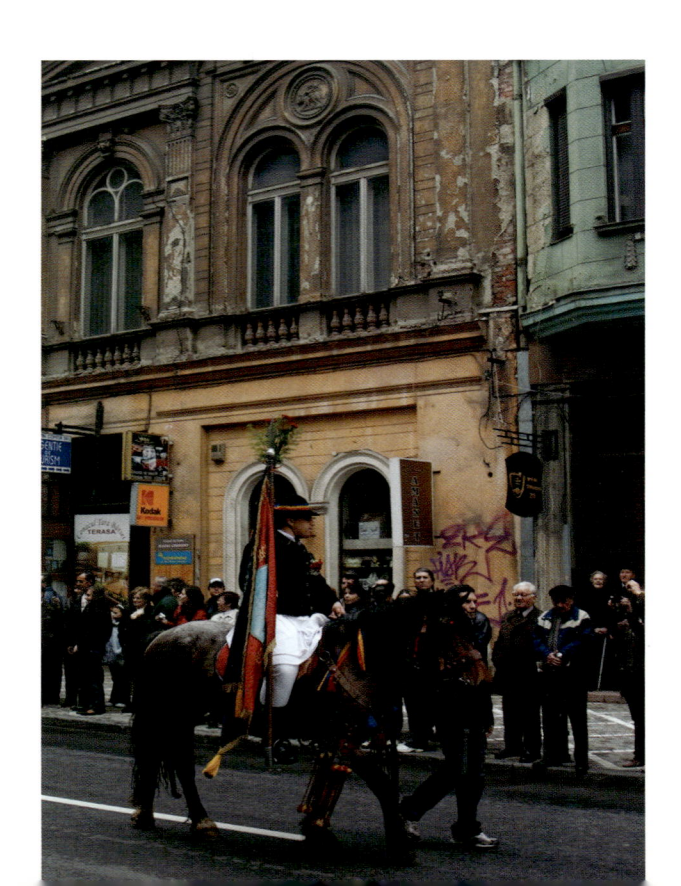

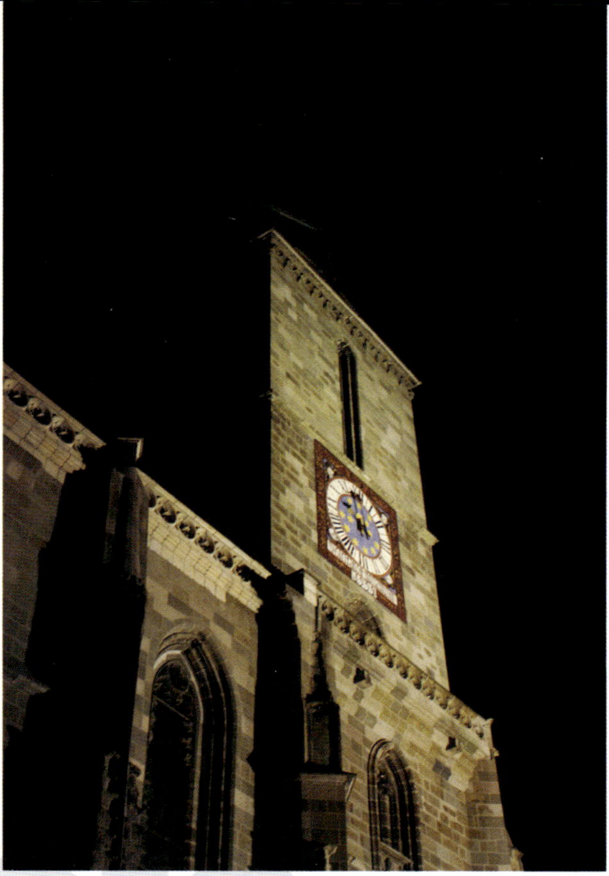

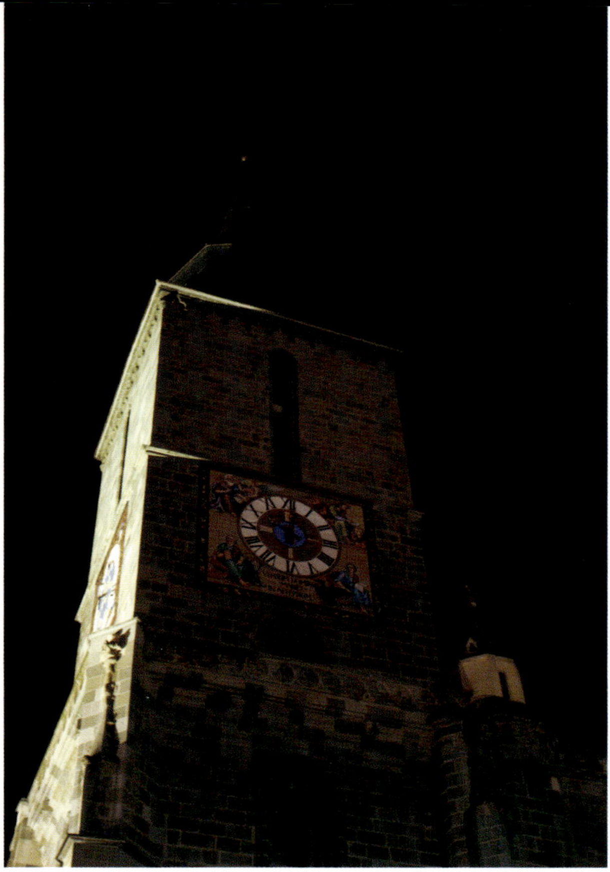

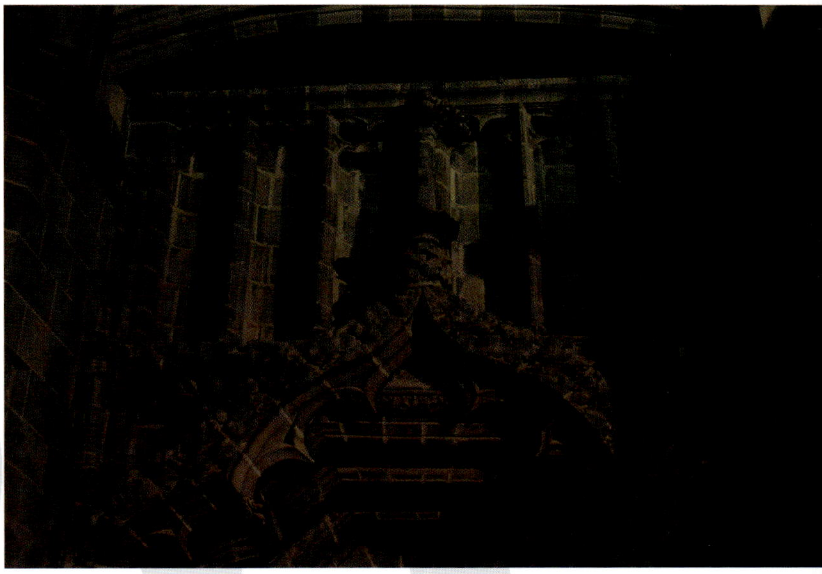

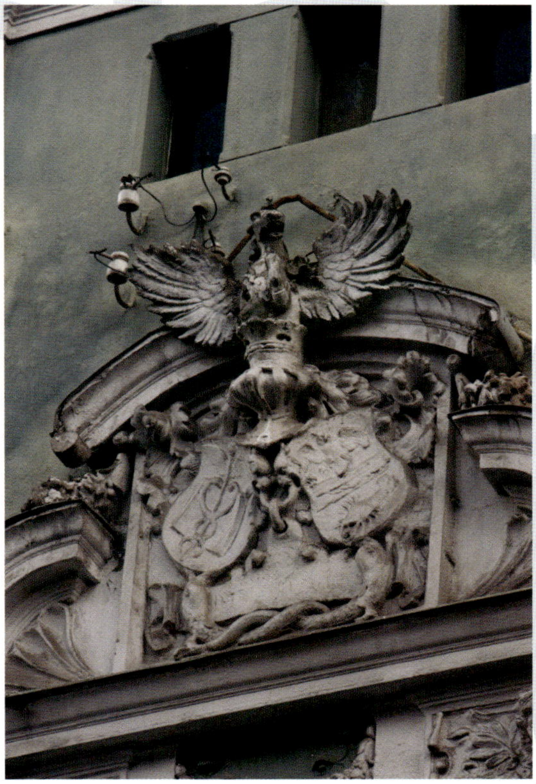

Hărman

Honigberg

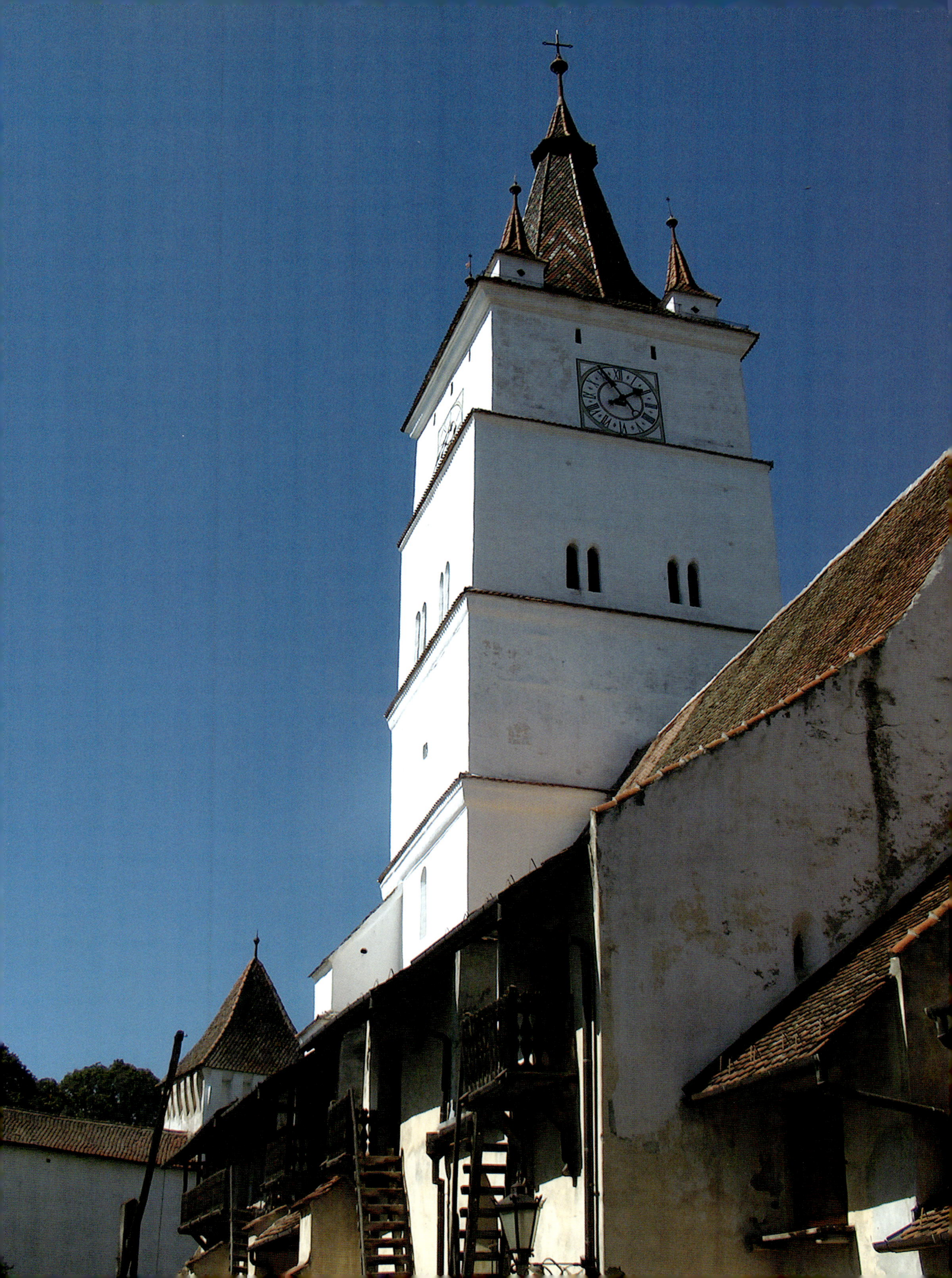

Prejmer

Tartlau

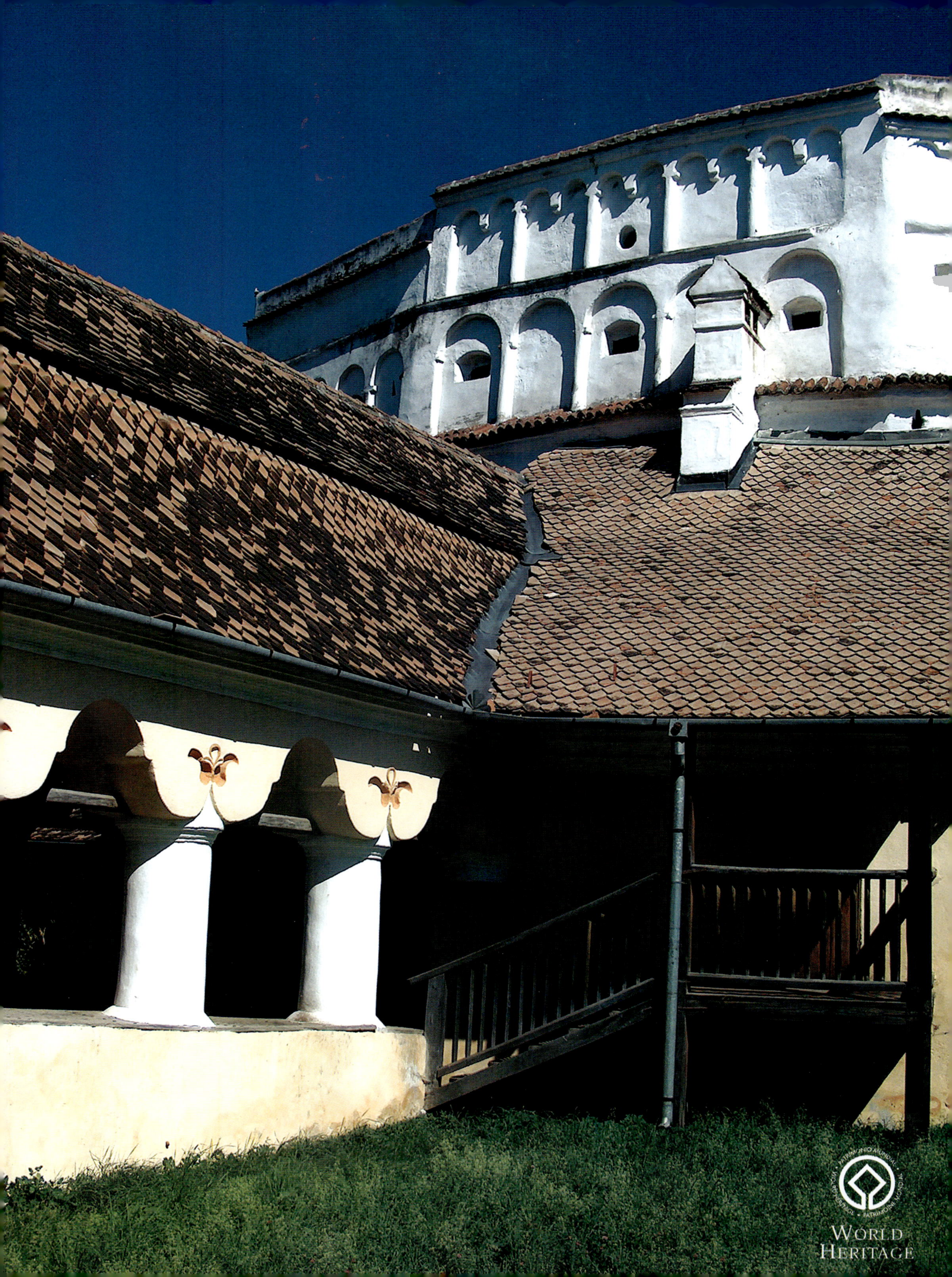
WORLD
HERITAGE

Rotbav

Rothbach

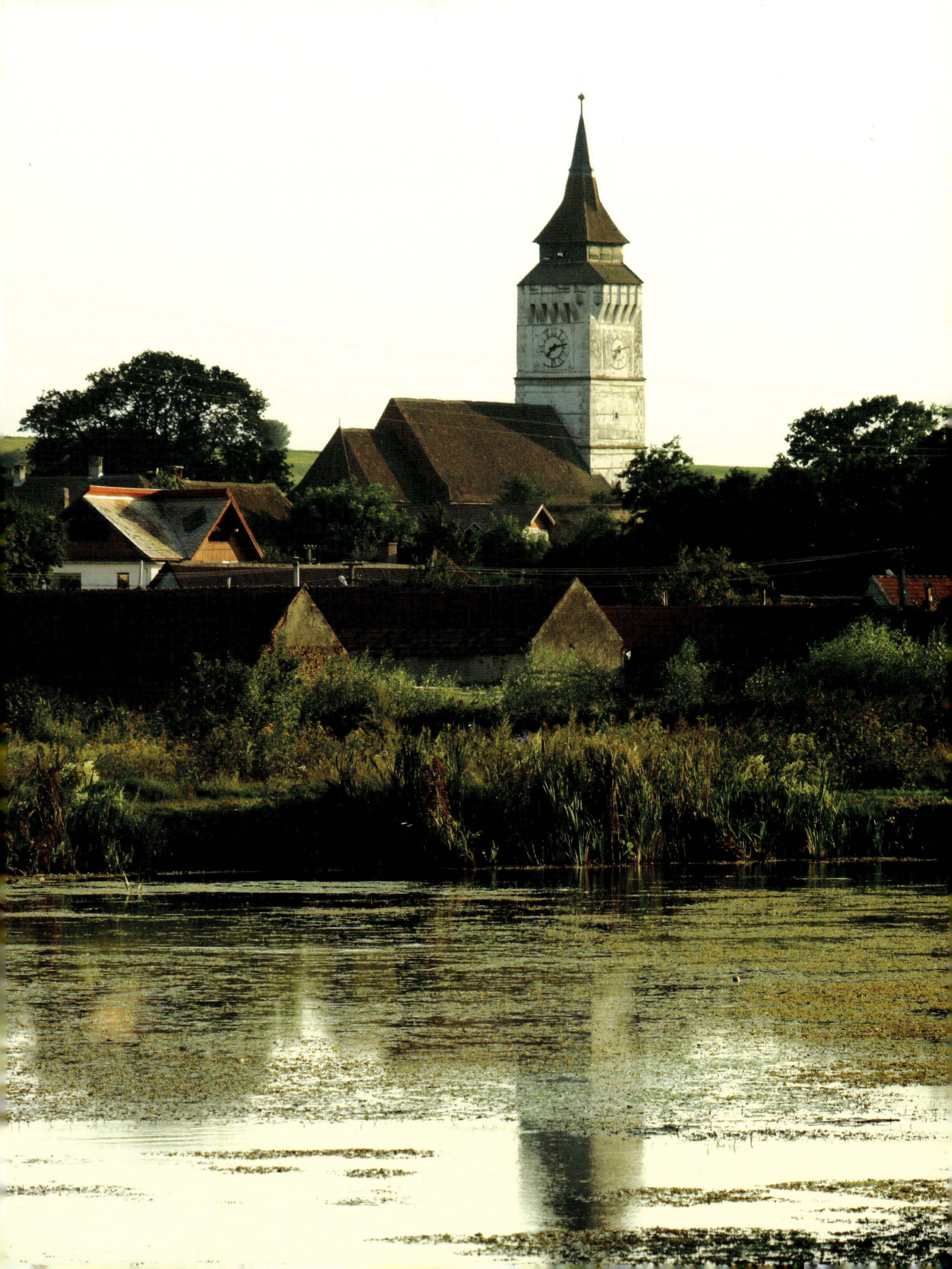

Cața

Katzendorf

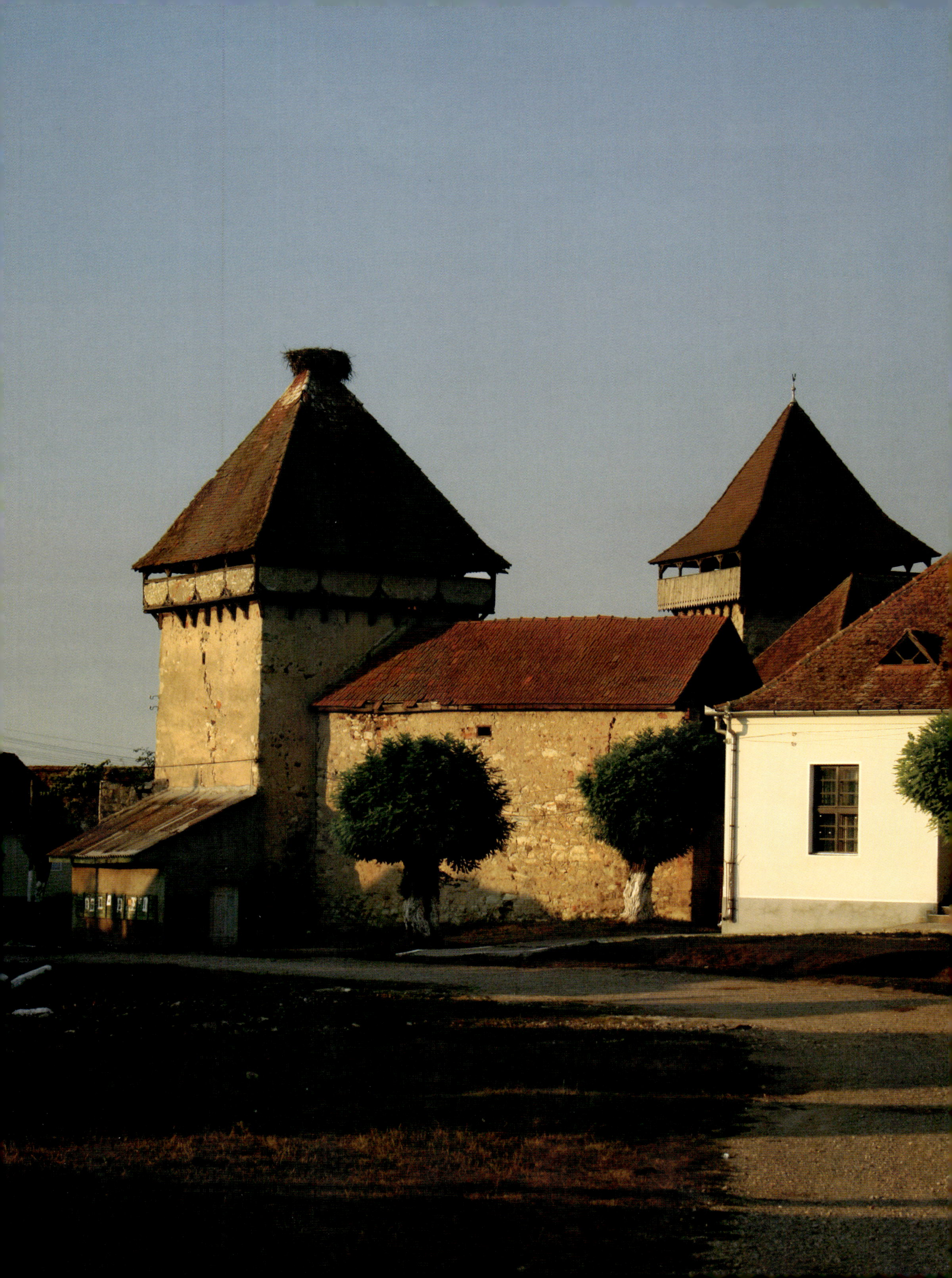

DRĂUȘENI
DRAAS

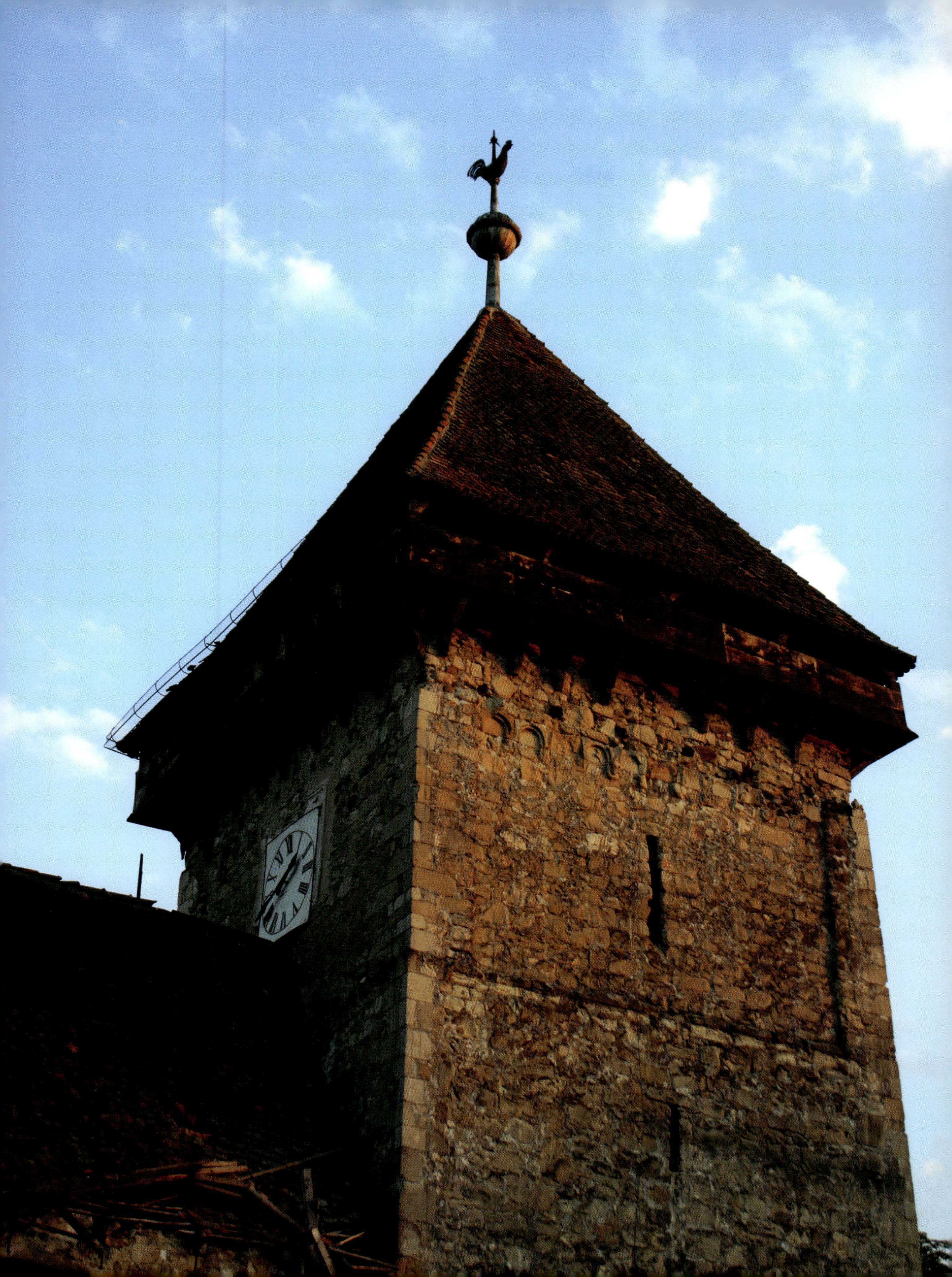

Homorod

Hamruden

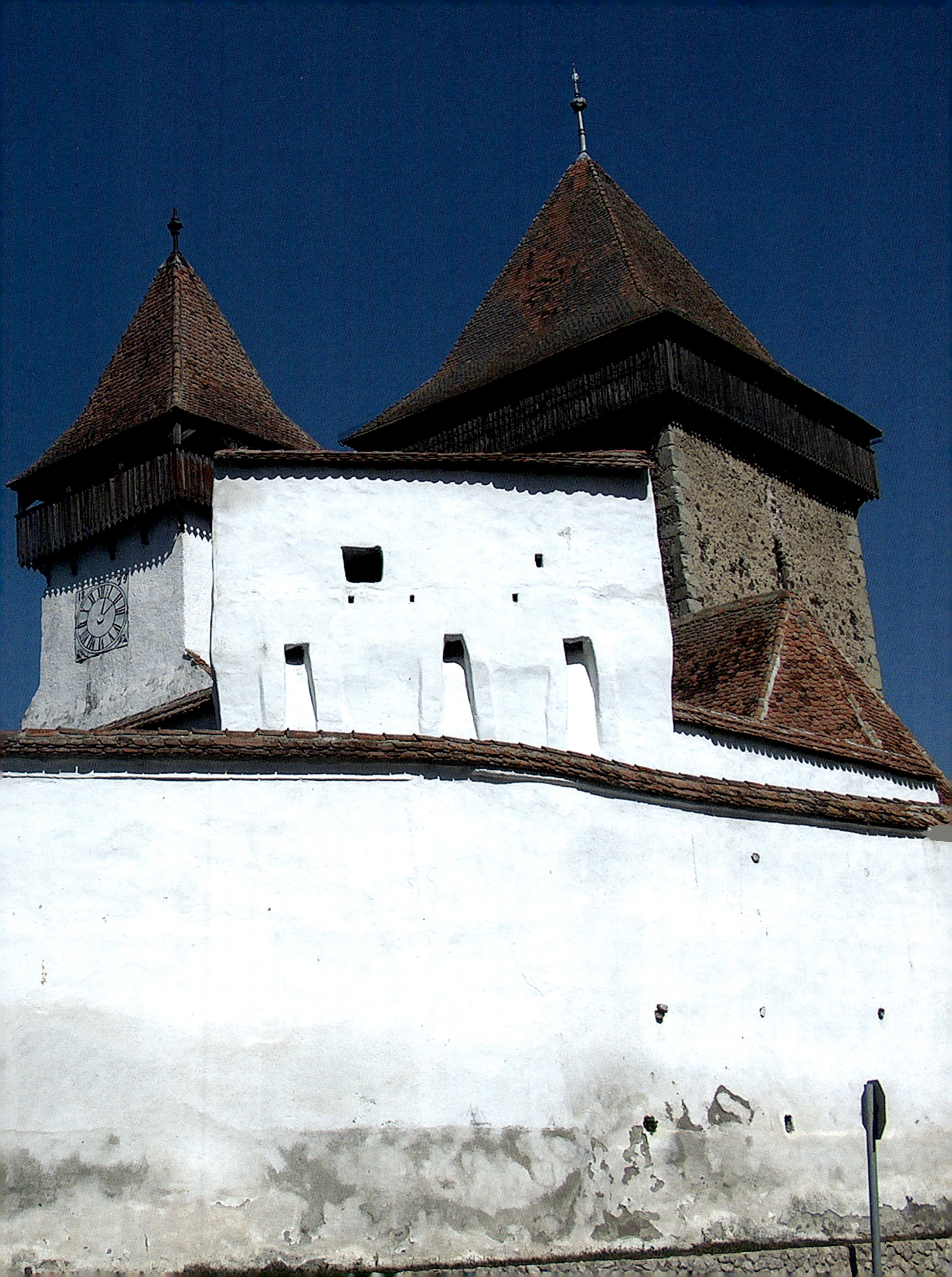

Buneşti
Bodendorf

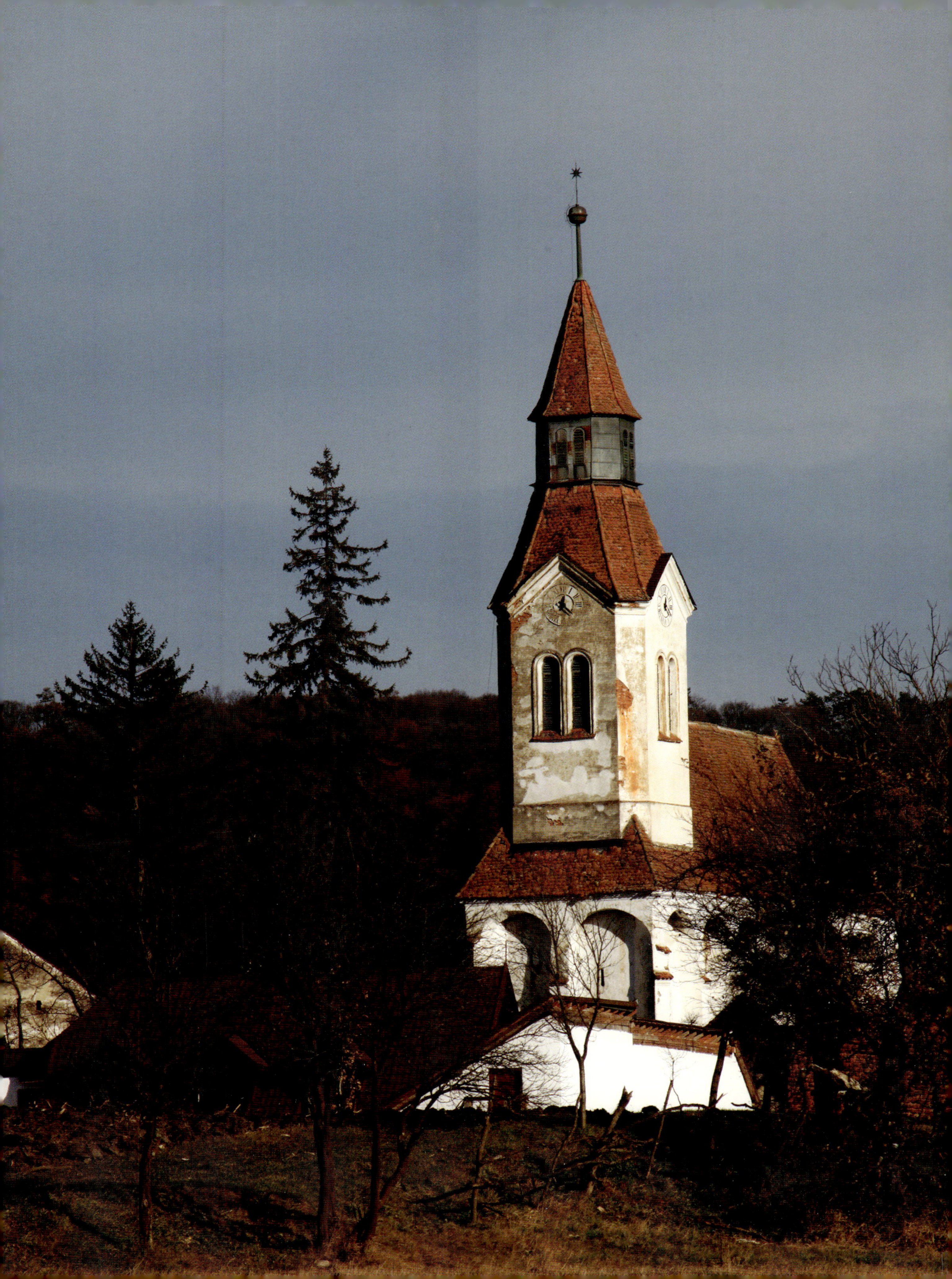

Viscri
Deutsch-Weißkirch

WORLD
HERITAGE

Meșendorf

Meschendorf

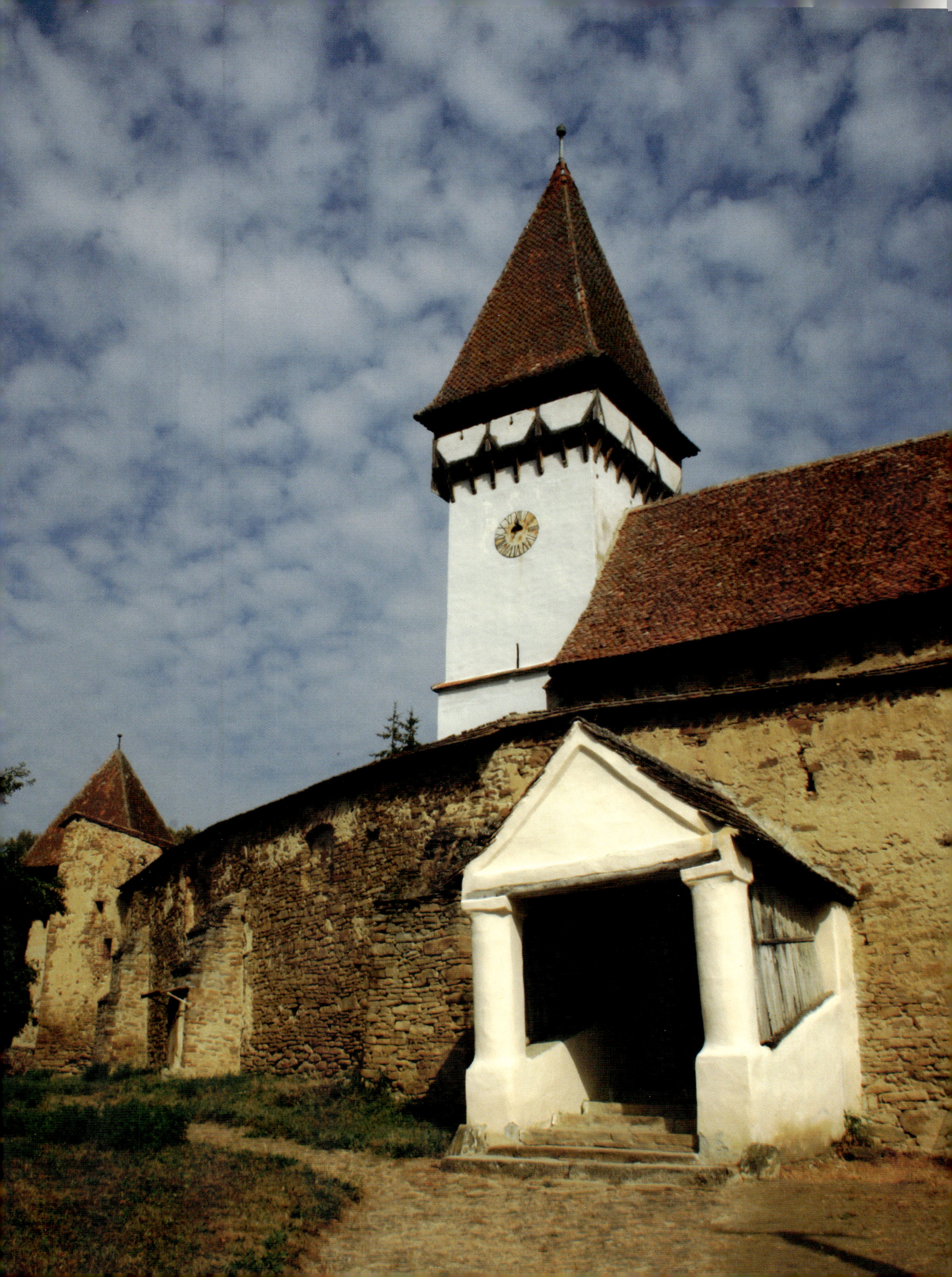

Criț
Deutschkreuz

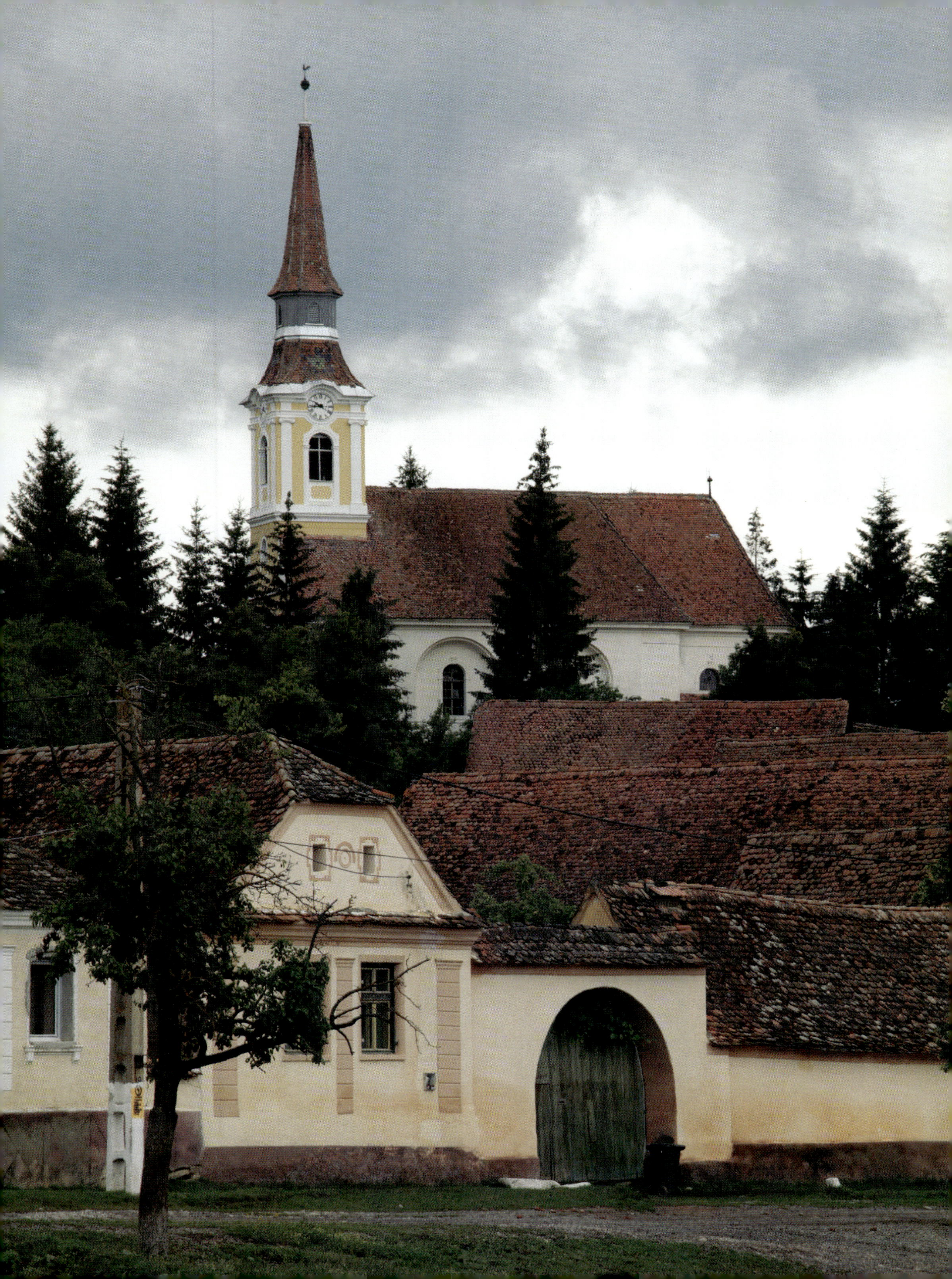

Marriage, Divorce and Ways of Persuasion

Nowadays we don't think of marriage as compulsory, not anymore. But back then, in a traditional society, un unmarried man/woman was incomplete; it was unthinkable!

And also the divorced man/woman was not well regarded.

Saxons had a particular way of dealing with the problem: if one couple was considering divorce, the community locked both of them in a very small room with a single bad, a single plate, one piece of bred, one cup for water; and they had to share everything for about 2 weeks in order to see if they can get back together.

Apparently this system really worked because it is said in the last 300 years there was one single divorce. Well...for sure there were other times!

In Biertan you can still see today one of these divorce rooms in one of the church wall's tower.

Die Eheschließung, das Zimmer gegen Ehescheidungen

Wir haben es aufgegeben, an die Eheschließung wie an ein Muss zu denken. Doch in einer traditionellen Gesellschaft wurde der Ledige wie ein unvollendeter Mensch betrachtet. Auch der Geschiedene ließ etwas, was er begonnen hatte, unvollendet. Bei den Sachsen beschloss die Gemeinde, im Falle, dass ein Ehepaar sich scheiden lassen wollte, dieses gemeinsam in ein kleines Gemach zu sperren, in dem es ein einziges Bett, einen einzigen Teller, ein einziges Besteck, ein Stück Brot und eine Kanne mit Wasser gab. Da mussten sie etwa zwei Wochen leben, genügend Zeit, um sich unter diesen Bedingungen wieder zusammen zu raufen. Es heißt, dass in den letzten 300 Jahren ein einziges Ehepaar nach den zwei Wochen der Zweisamkeit dennoch die Trennung beantragte. In Birthälm kann man dieses Gemach noch sehen, es befindet sich in einer der Basteien der Kirchenburg.

Sighișoara – Mediaș

→ Saschiz (Keisd)

← Cloașterf (Klosdorf)

→ Archita (Arkeden)

→ Sighișoara (Schäßburg)

← Apold (Trappold)

← Daia (Denndorf)

→ Daneș (Dunesdorf)

← Seleuș (Groß-Alisch)

→ Laslea (Großlasseln)

← Mălâncrav (Malmkrog)

→ Valchid (Waldhütten)

← Copșa Mare (Großkopisch)

→ Biertan (Birthälm)

→ Richiș (Reichesdorf)

→ Alma Vii (Almen)

→ Moșna (Meschen)

→ Brateiu (Pretai)

← Dârlos (Durles)

→ Curciu (Kirtsch)

← Băgaciu (Bogeschdorf)

→ Velț (Wölz)

← Bazna (Baaßen)

← Mediaș (Mediasch)

← Valea Viilor (Wurmloch)

← Ighișu Nou (Eibesdorf)

← Axente Sever (Frauendorf)

Saschiz
Keisd

WORLD
HERITAGE

Cloașterf
Klosdorf

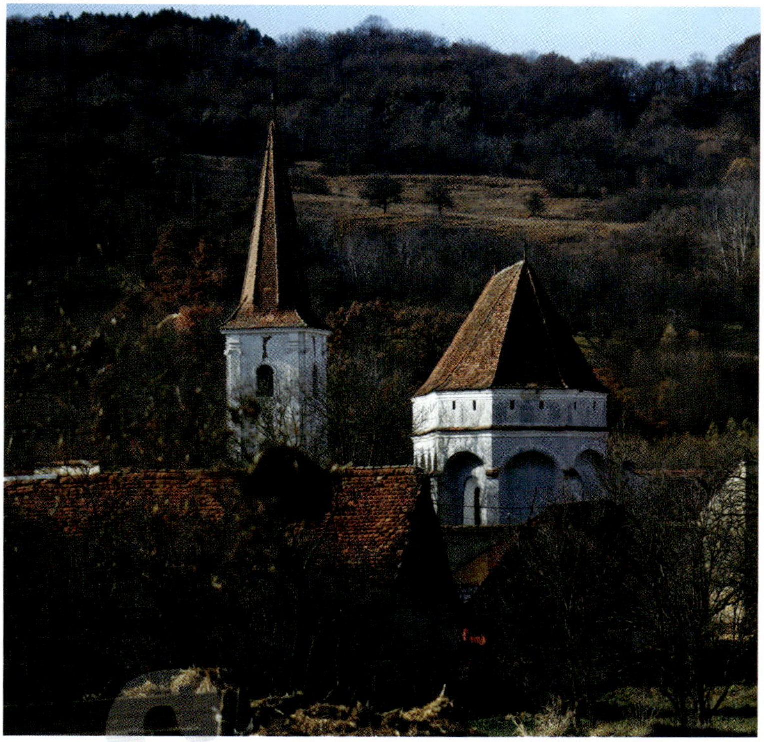
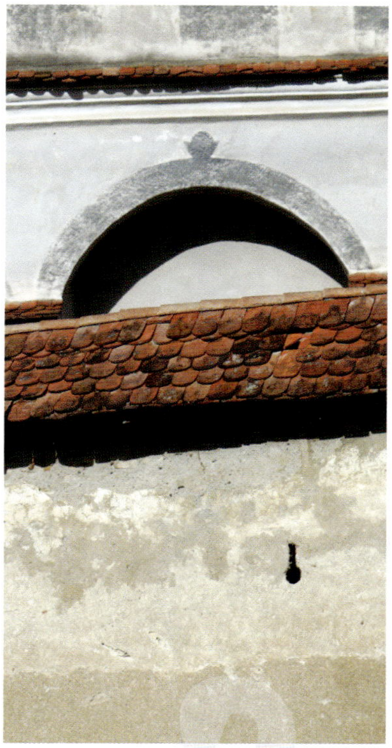
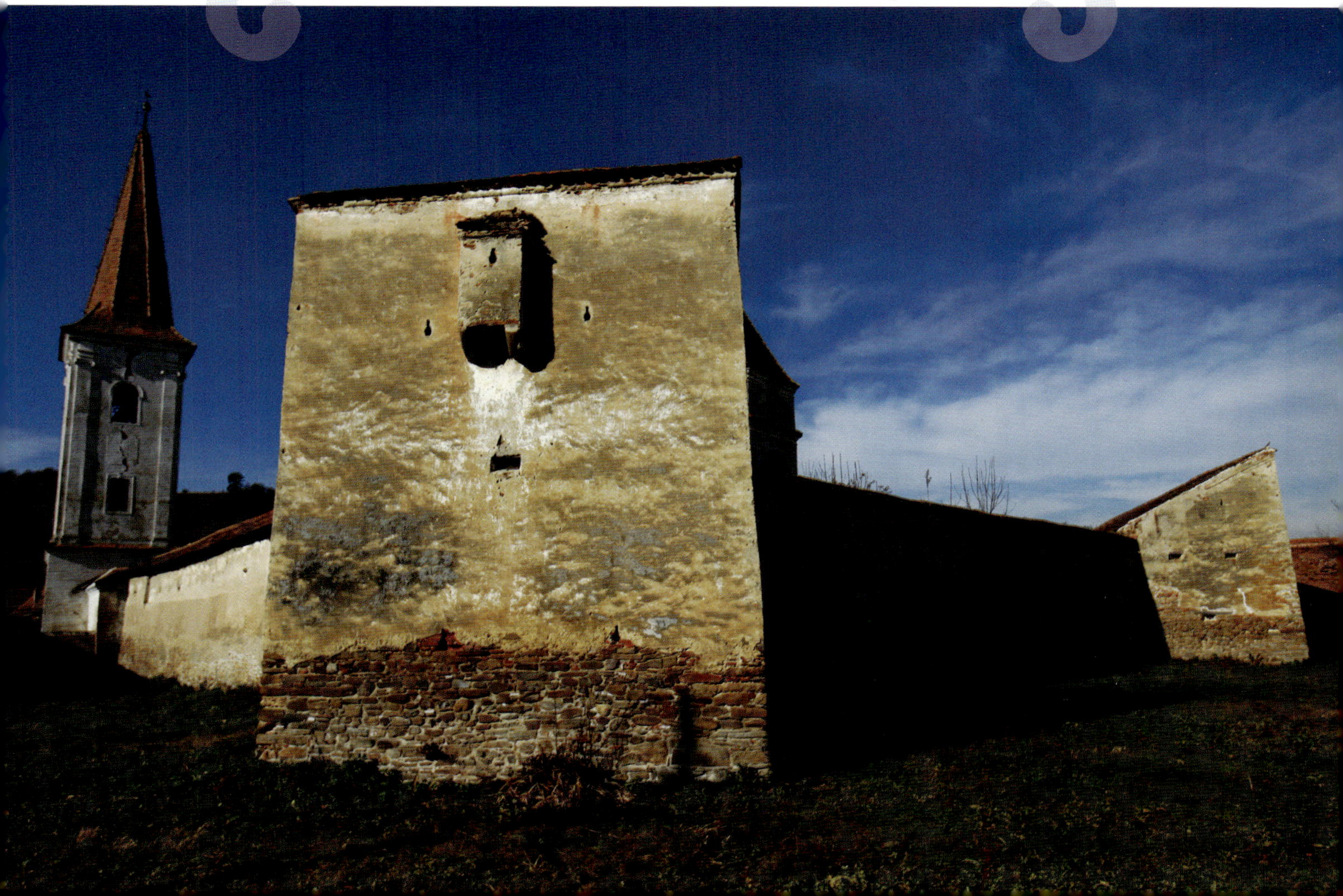

Archita
Arkeden

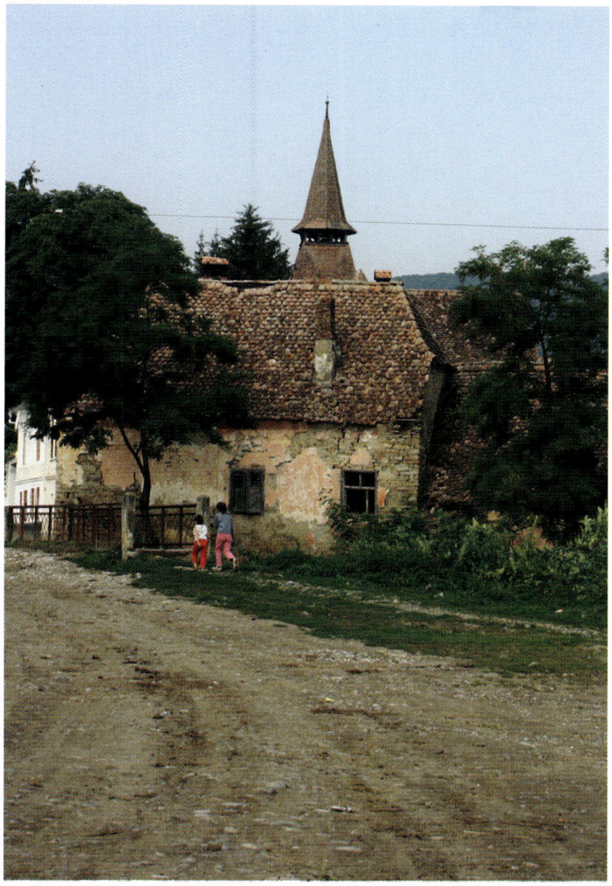

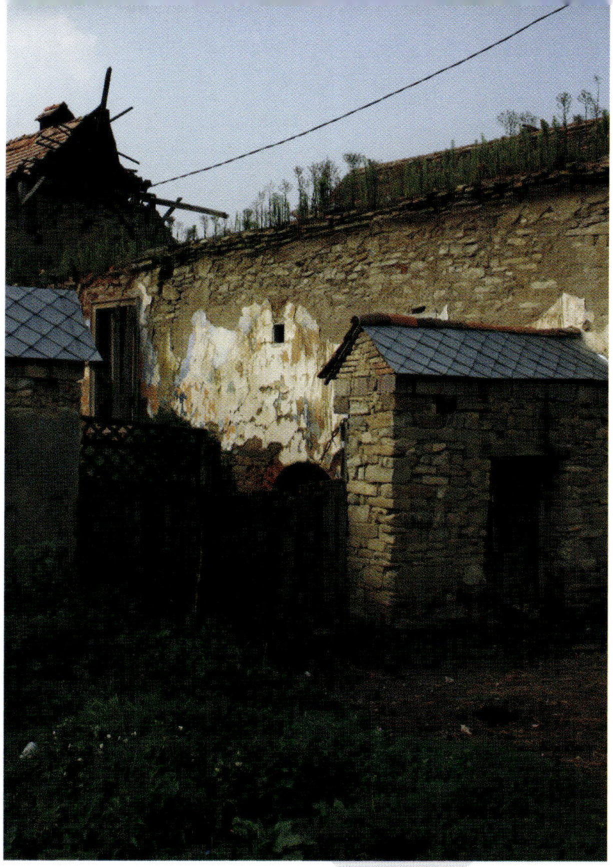

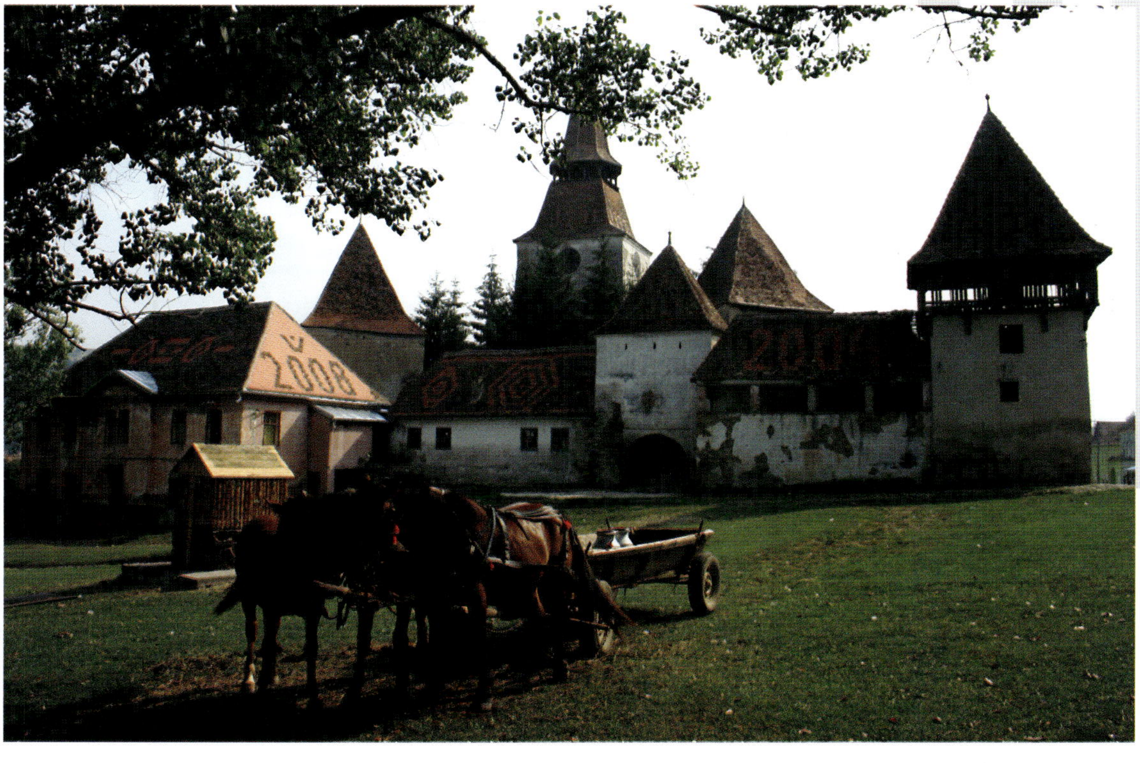
2008

Sighișoara

Schäßburg

WORLD
HERITAGE

APOLD
TRAPPOLD

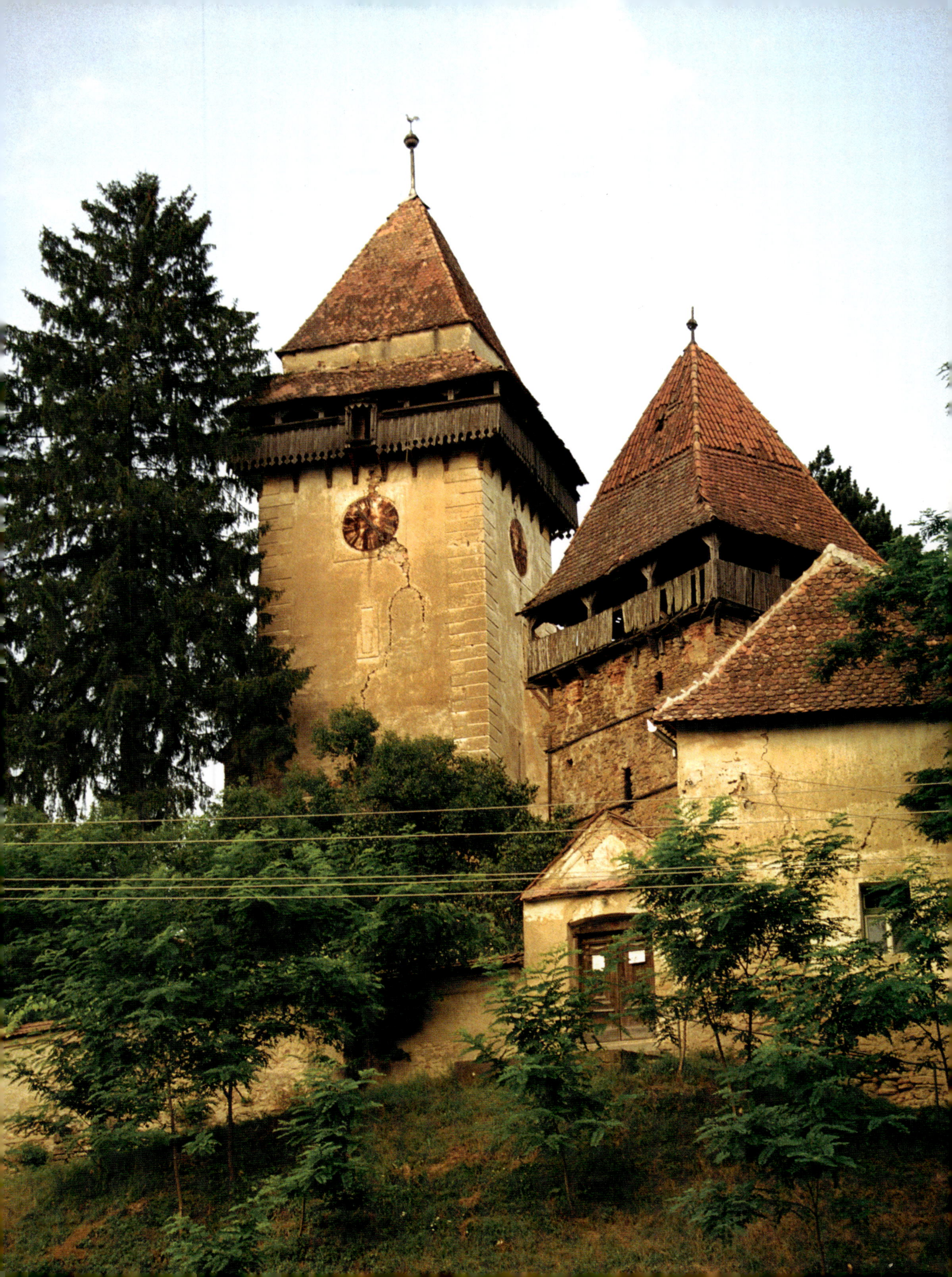

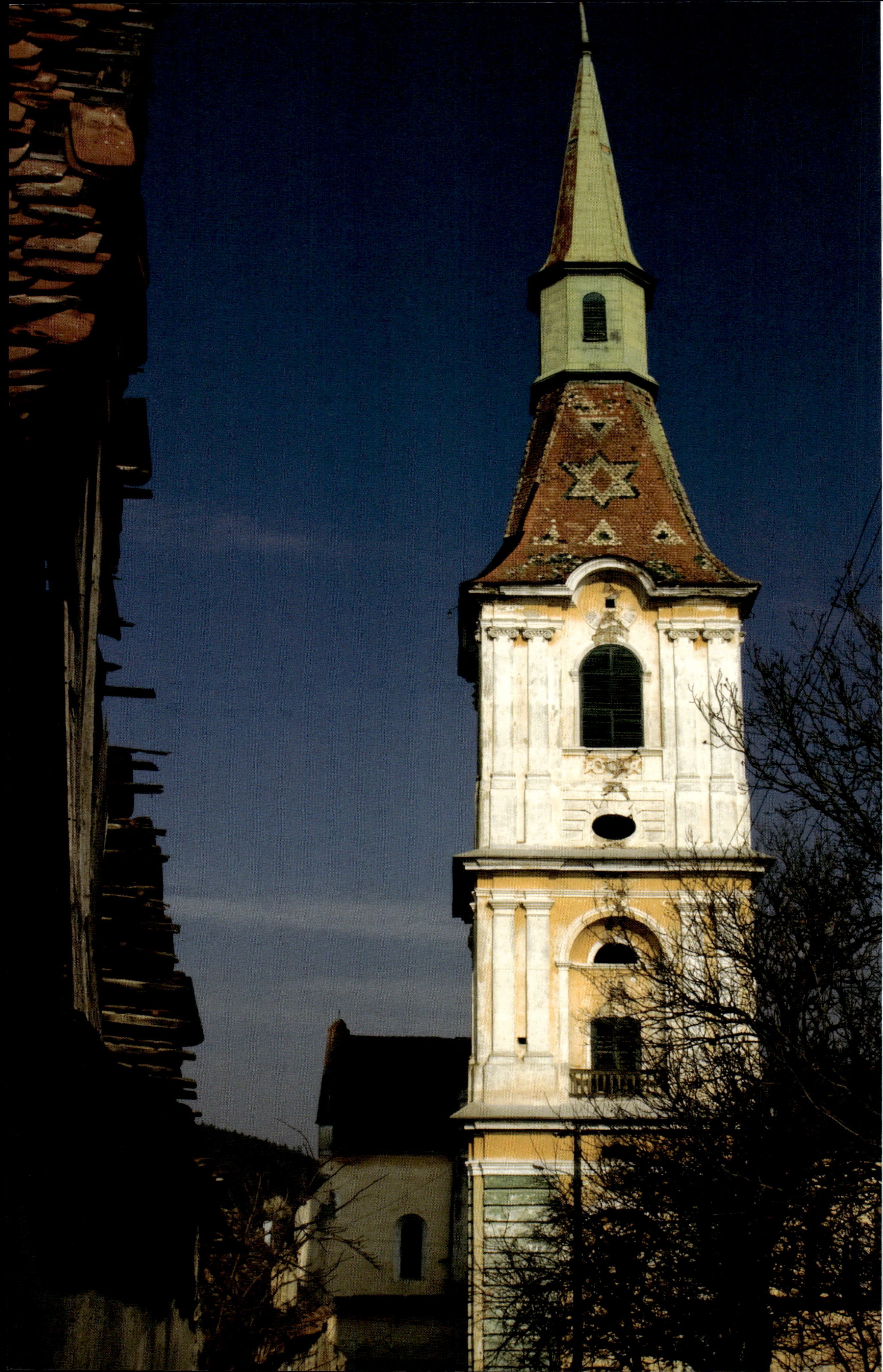

Daia
Denndorf

Daneş
Dunesdorf

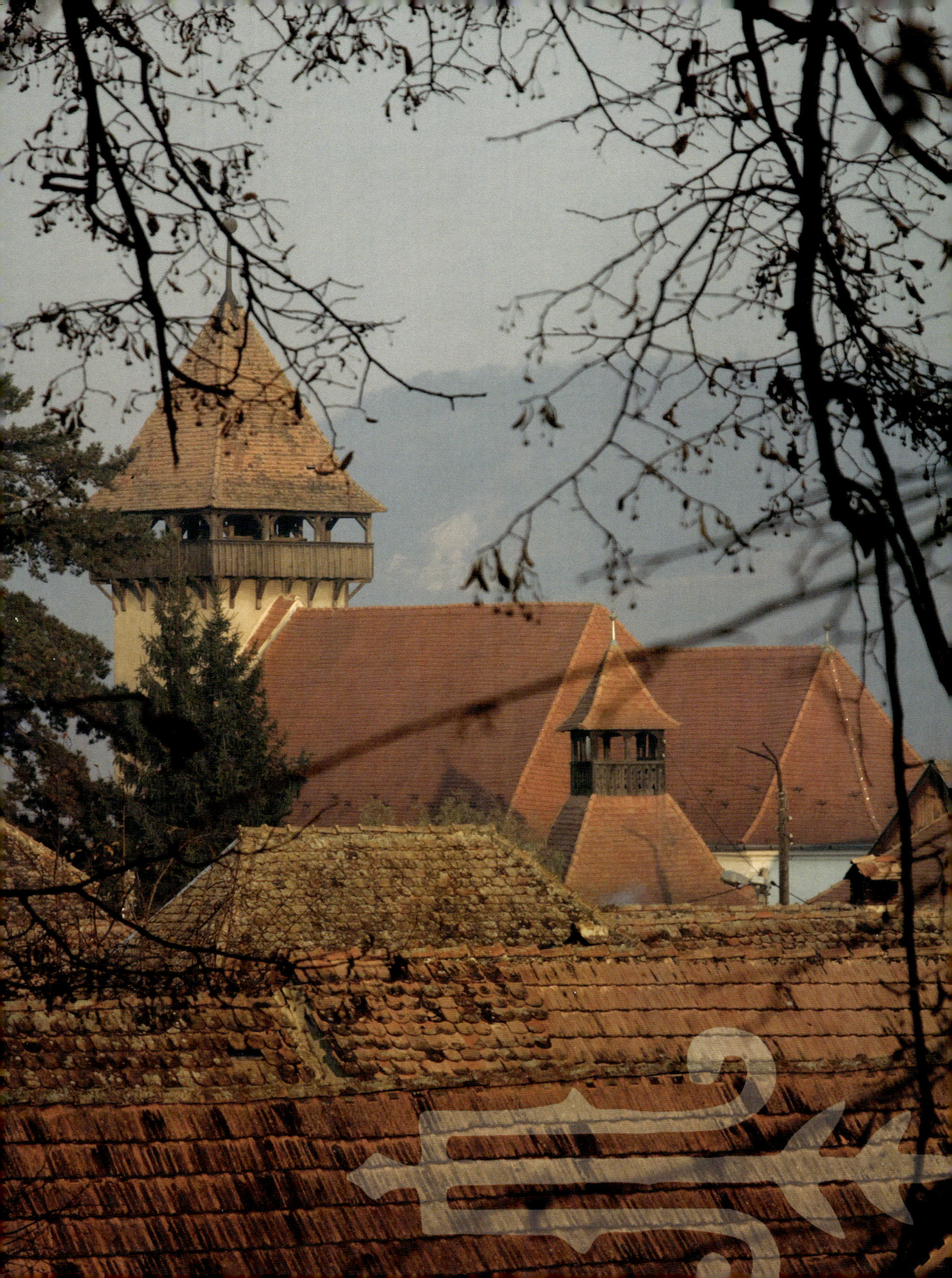

Seleuş
Groß - Alisch

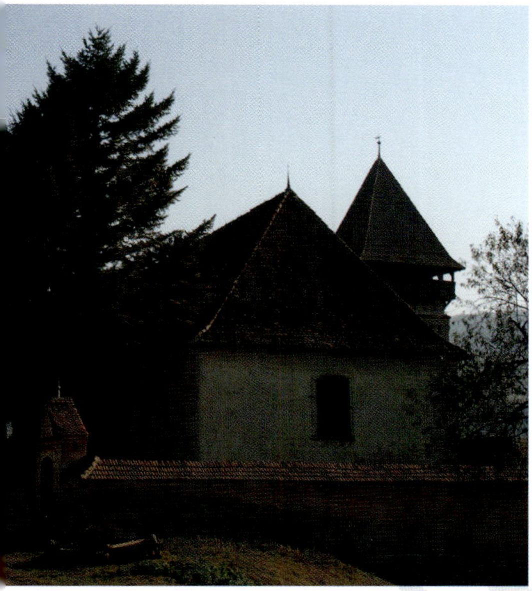
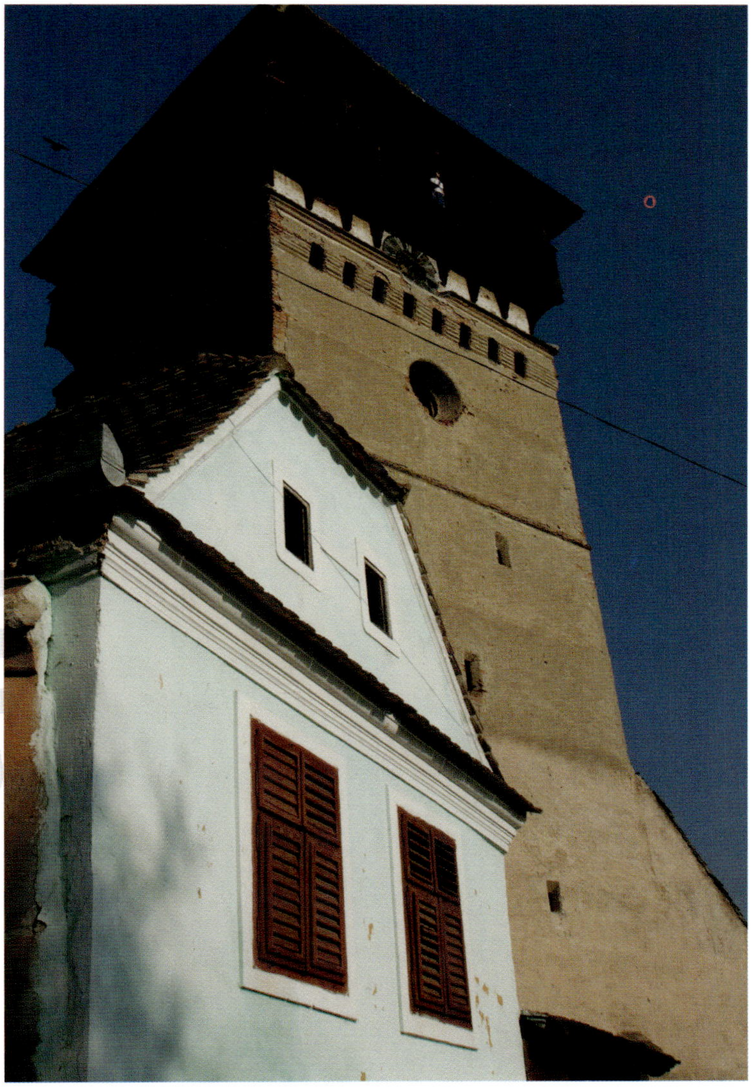
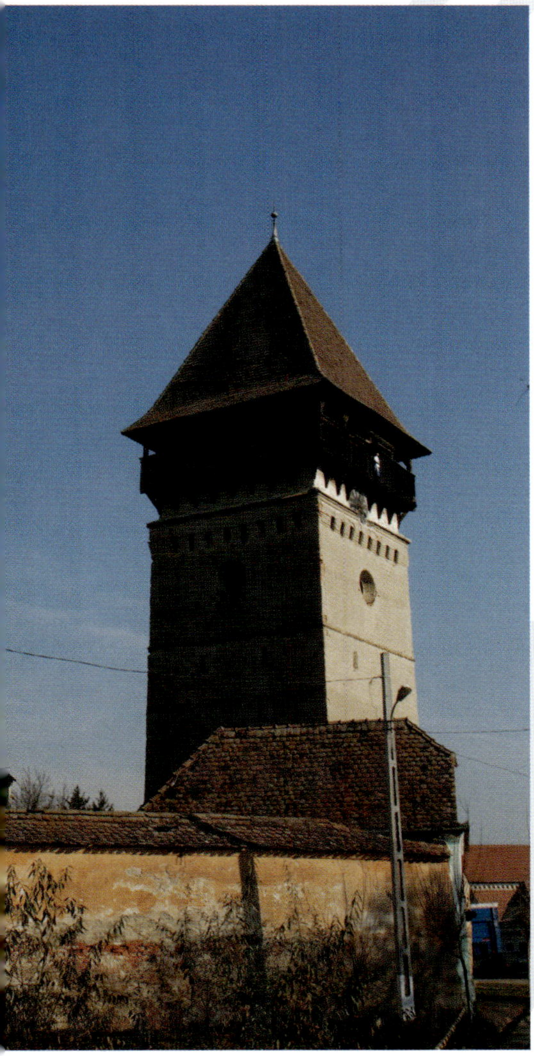
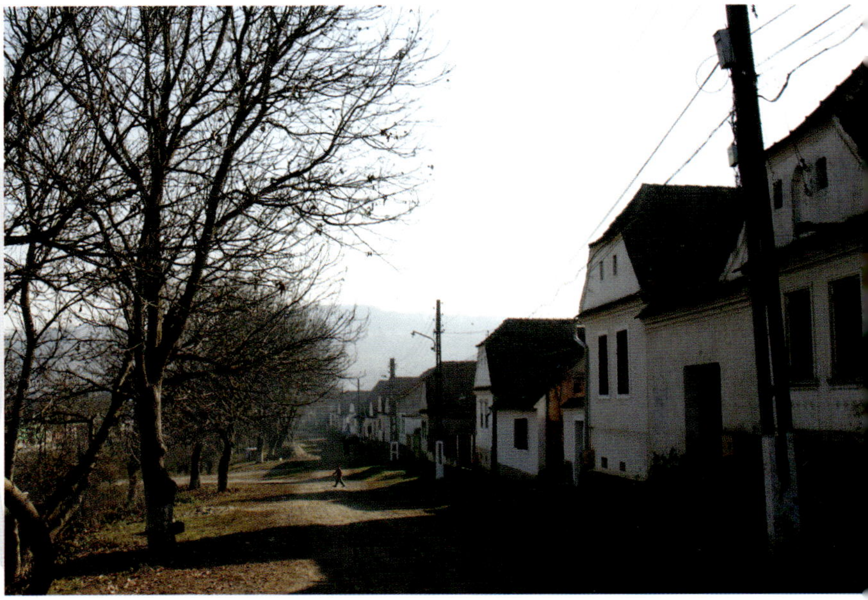

Laslea
Großlasseln

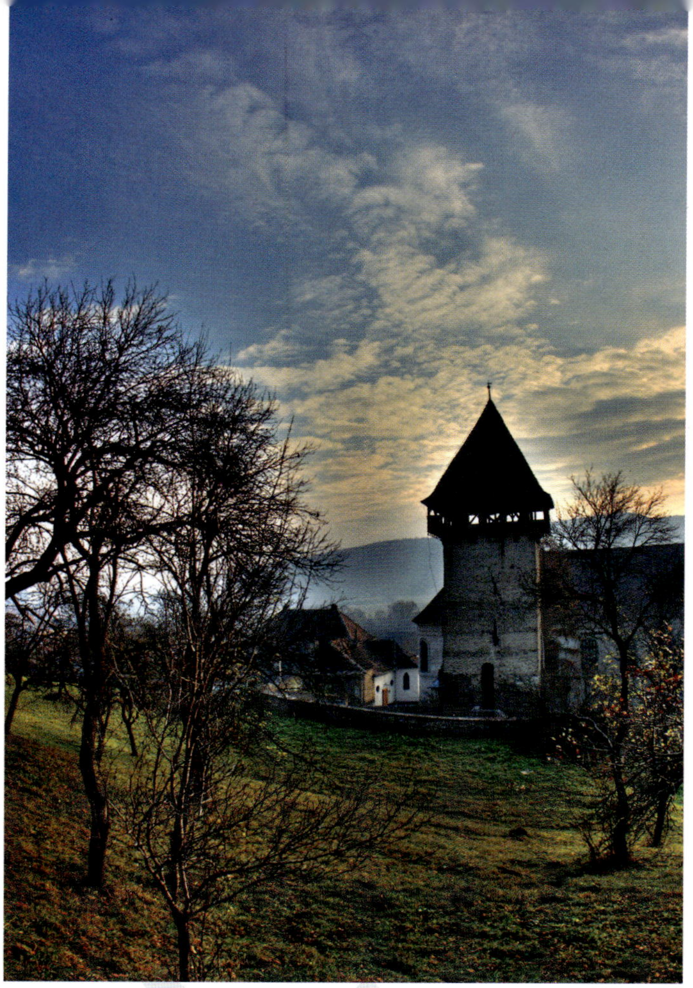

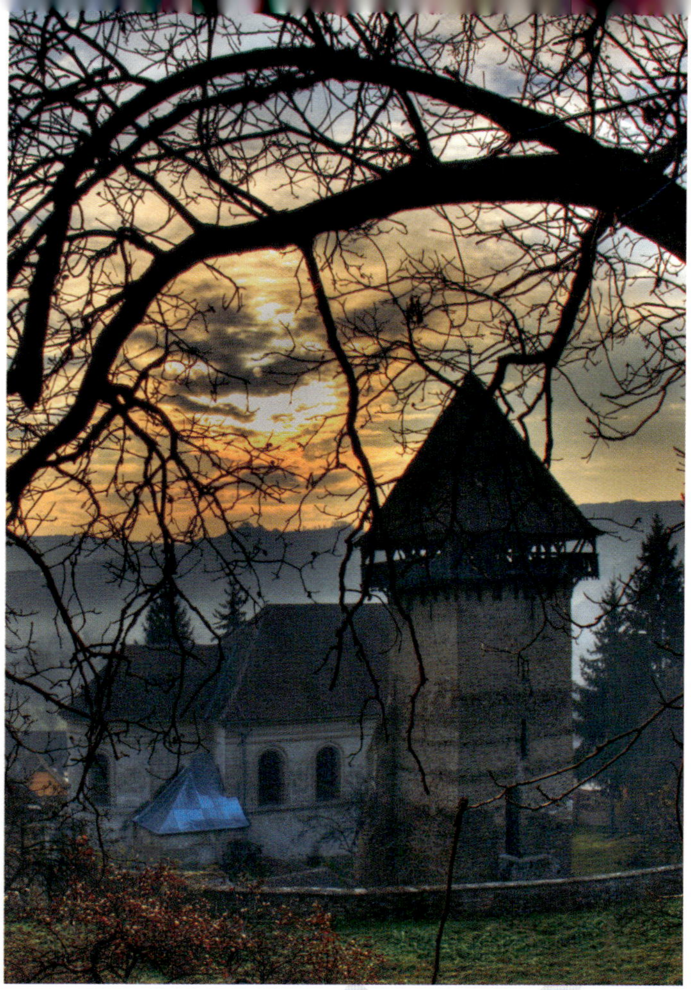

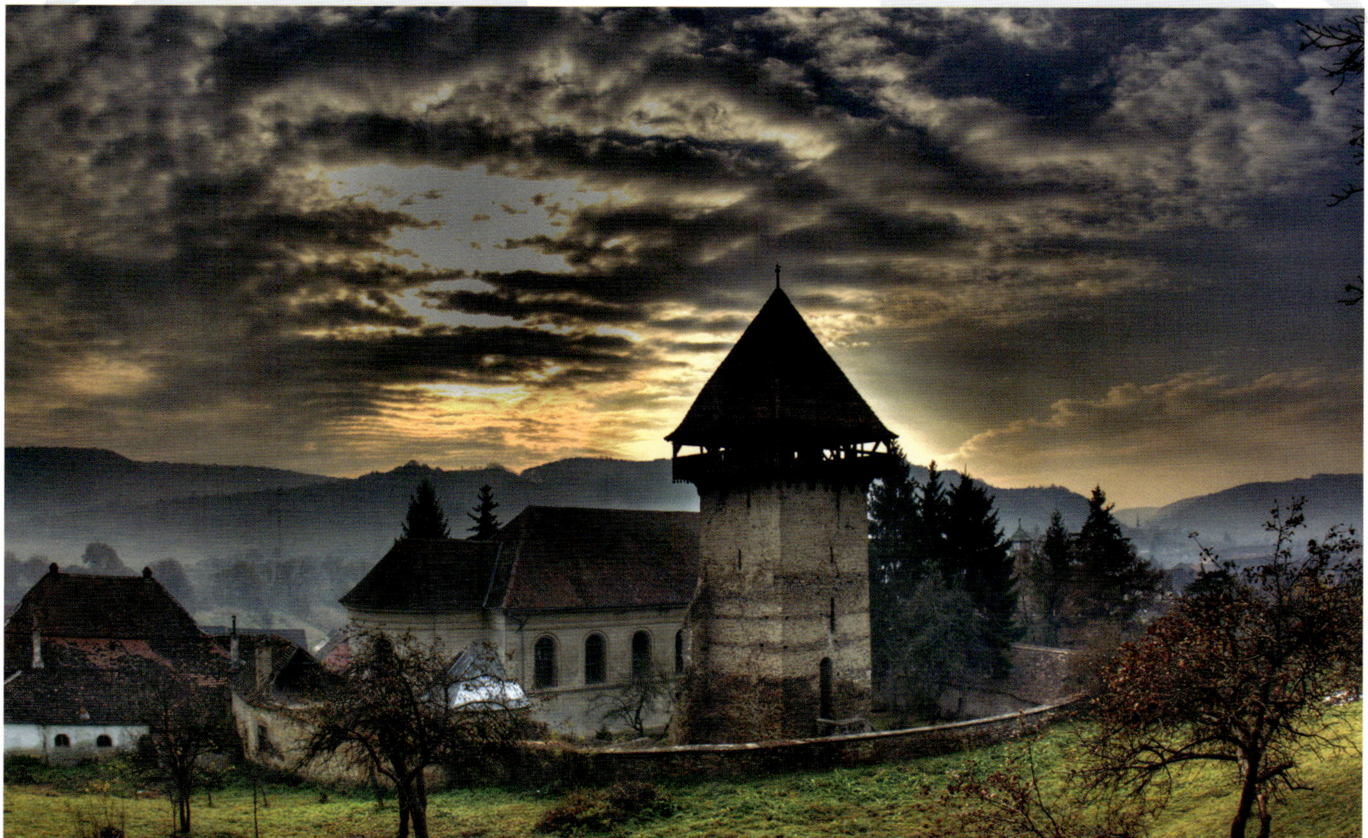

MĂLÂNCRAV
MALMKROG

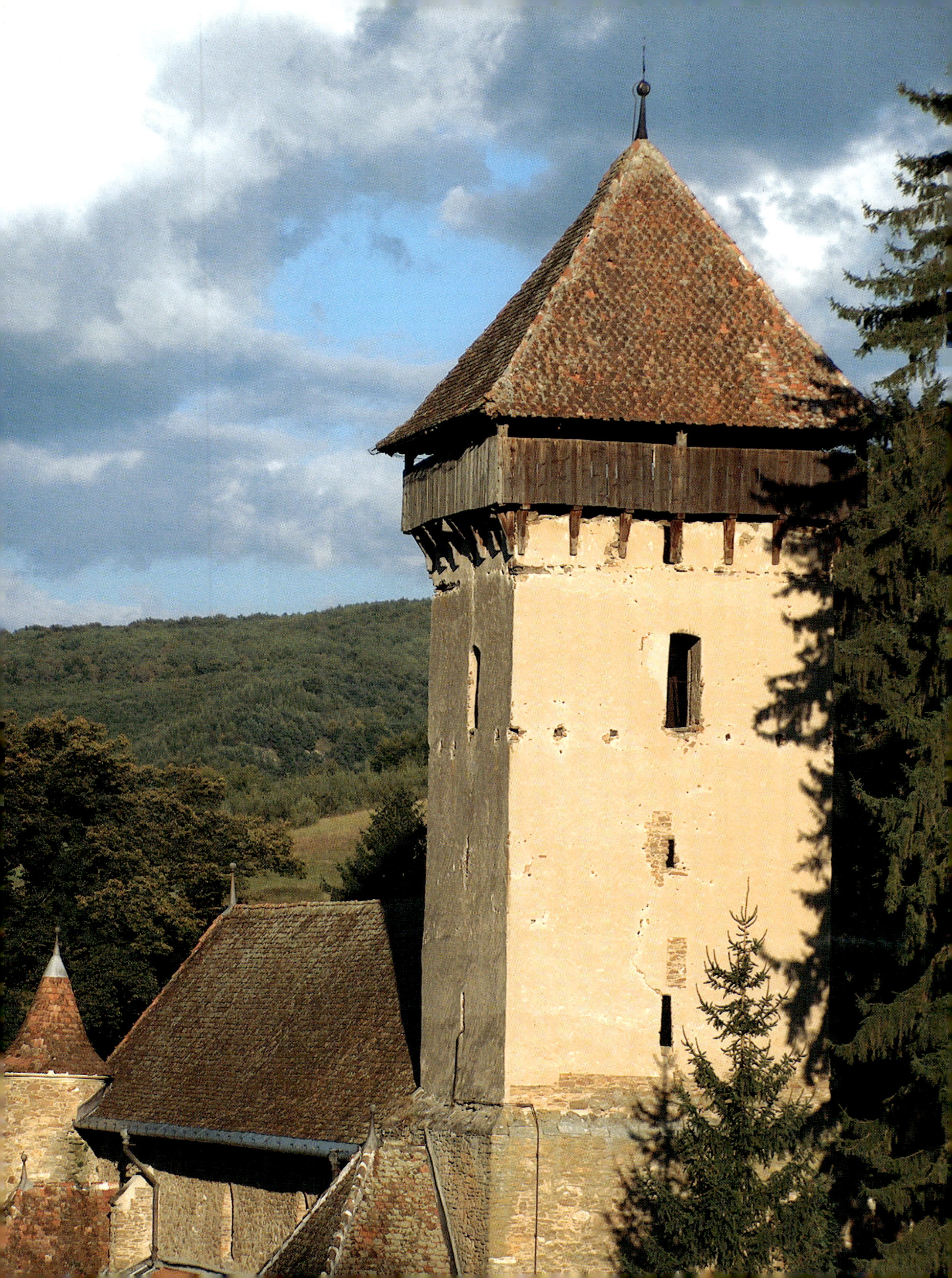

Valchid

Waldhütten

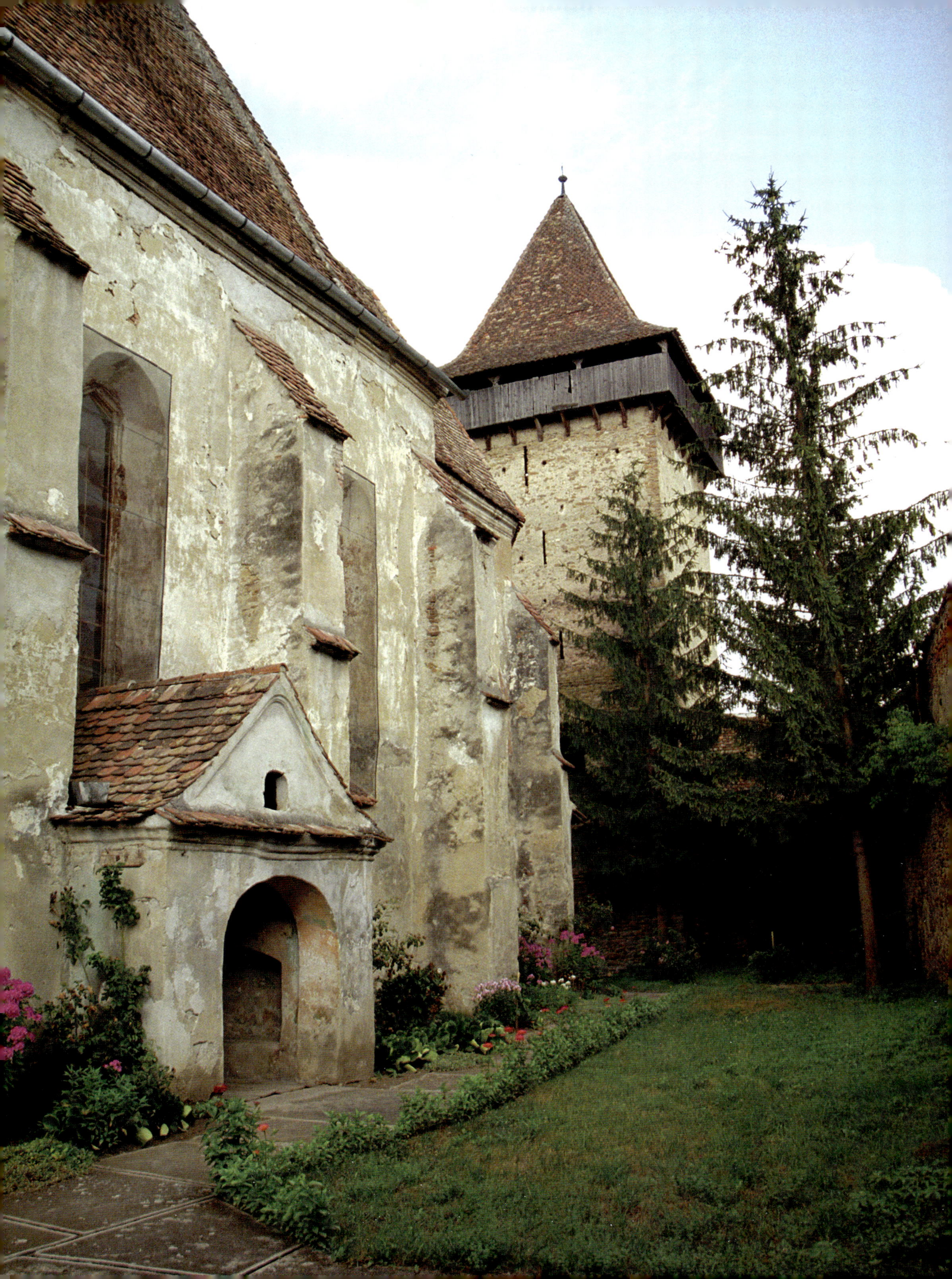

Copșa Mare
Großkopisch

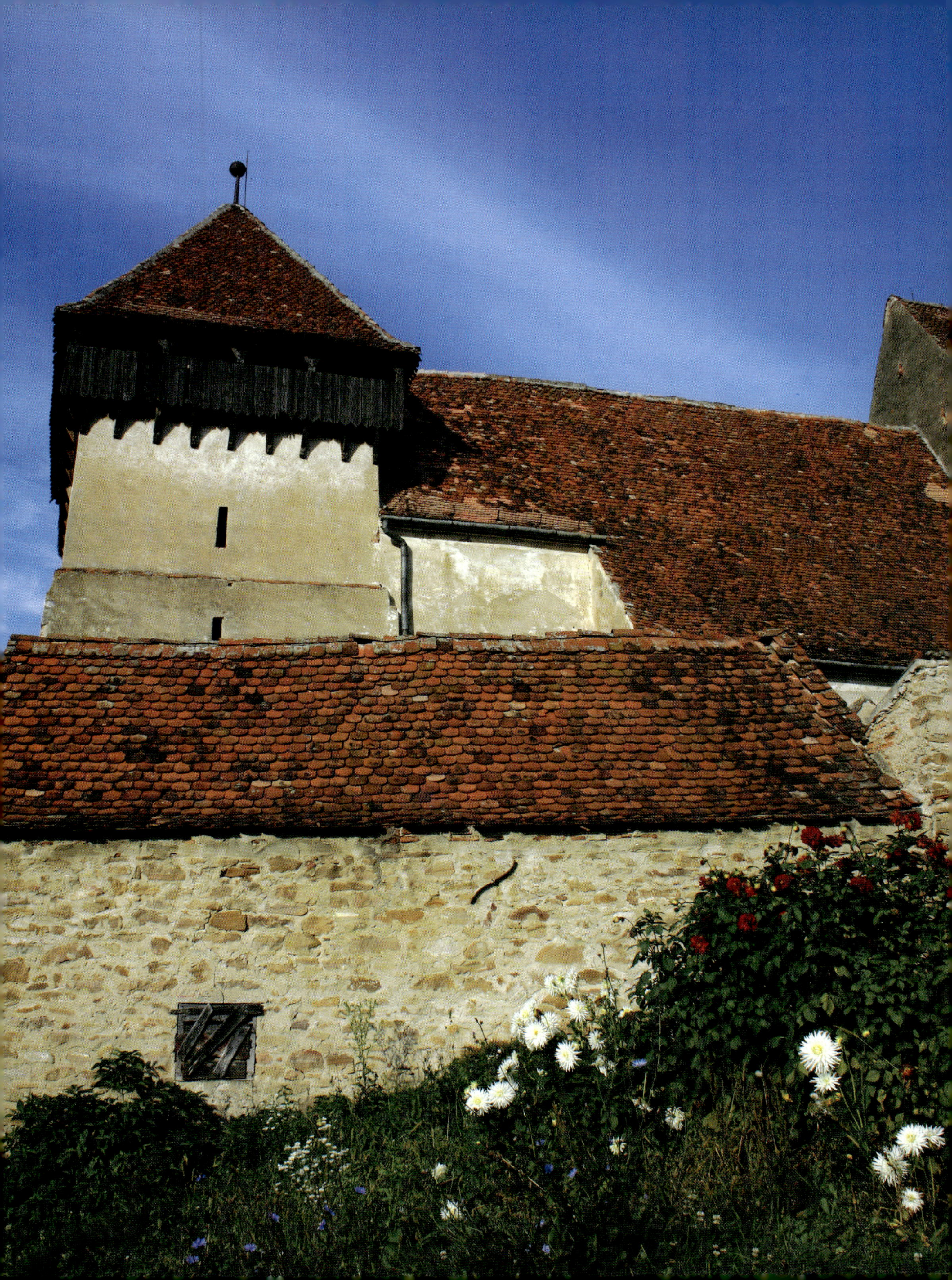

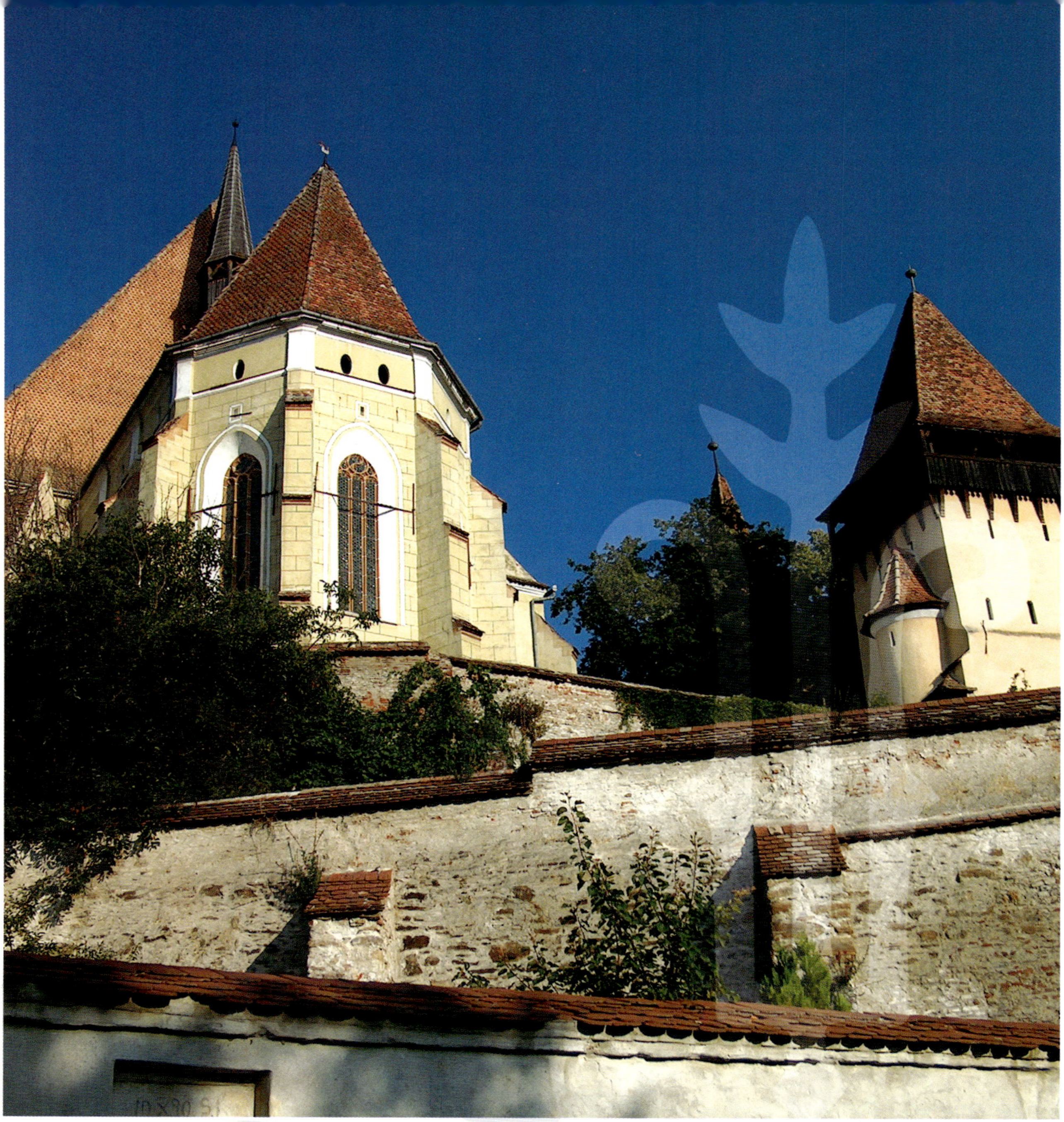

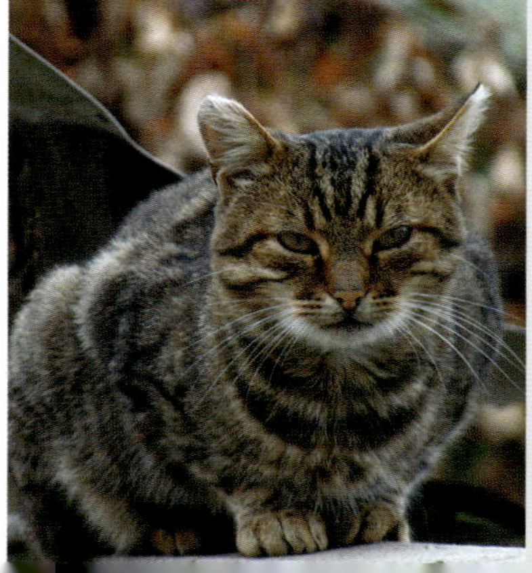

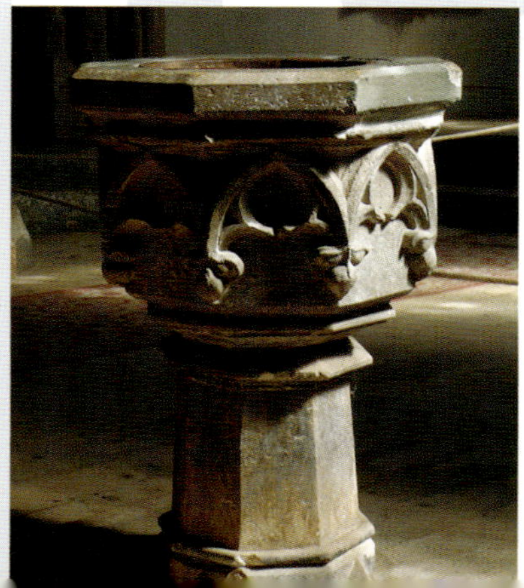

Biertan
Birthälm

WORLD HERITAGE

Richiş
Reichesdorf

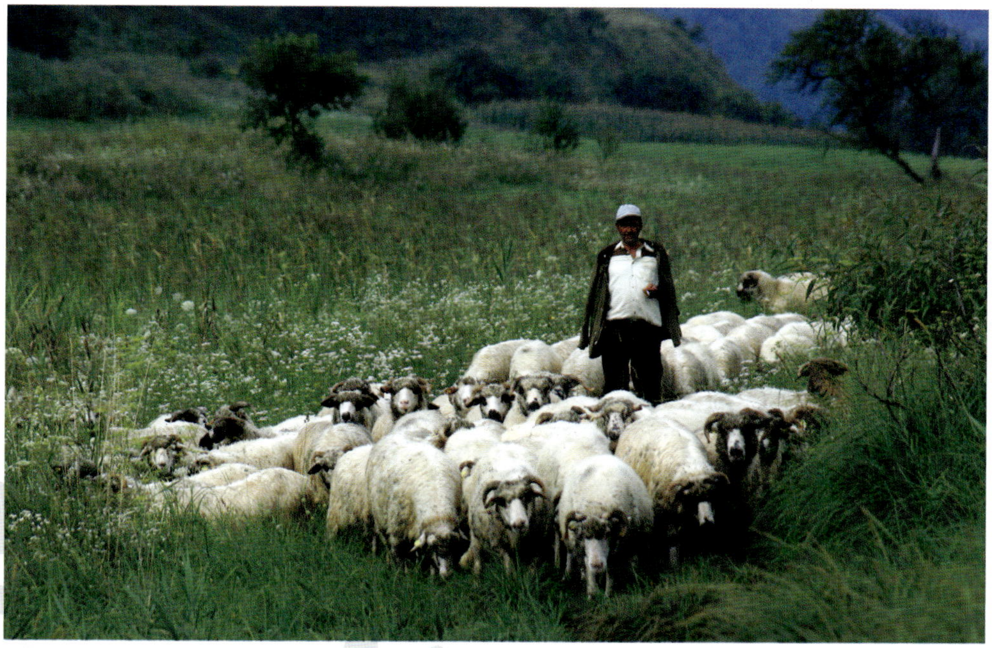

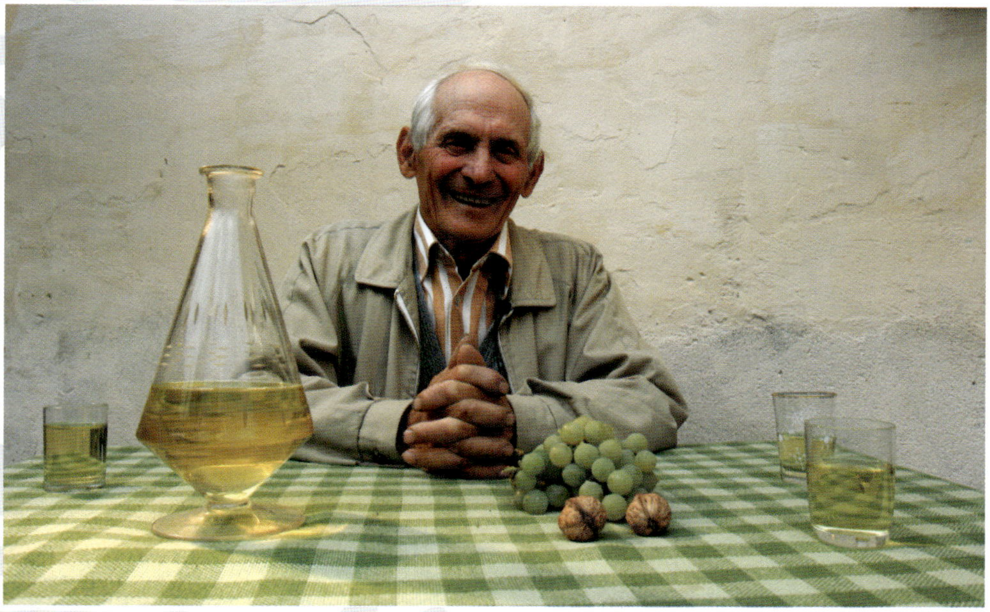

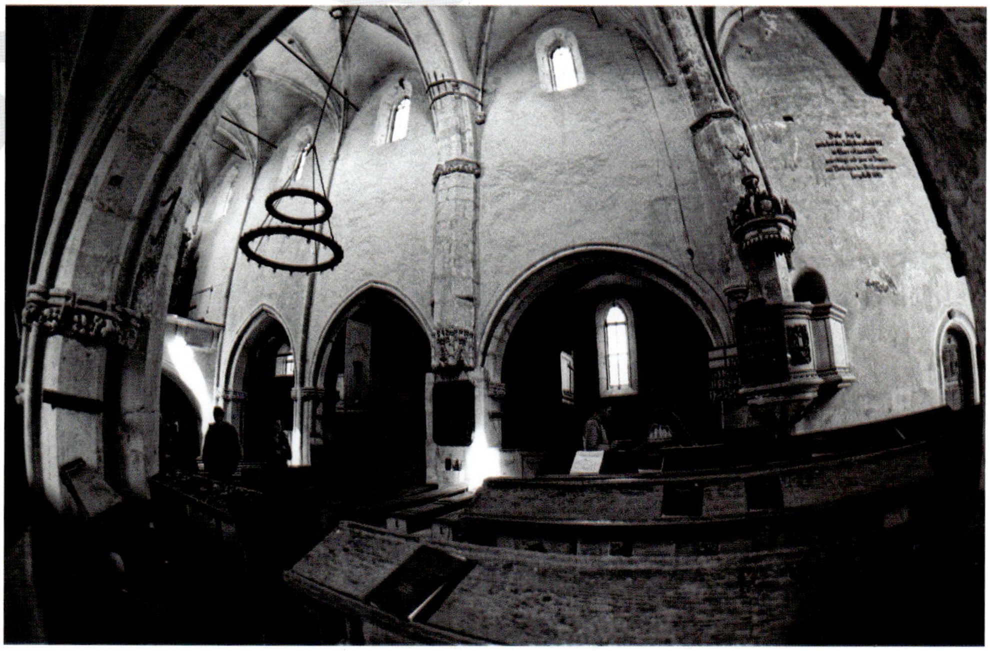

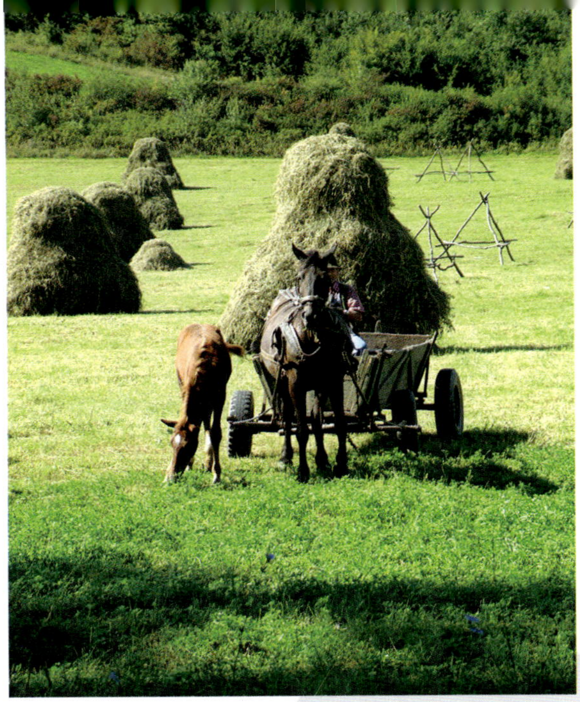

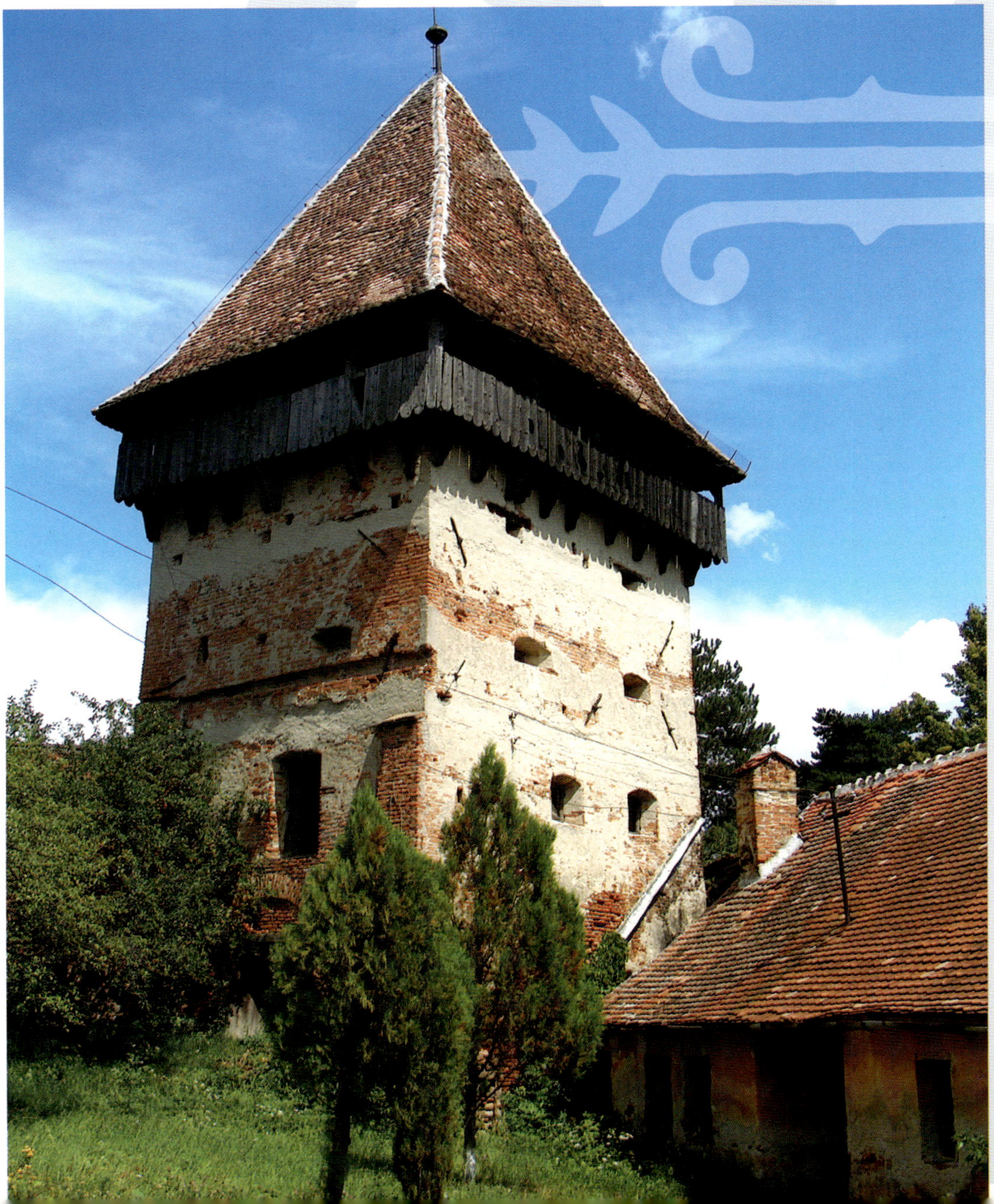

Alma Vii
Almen

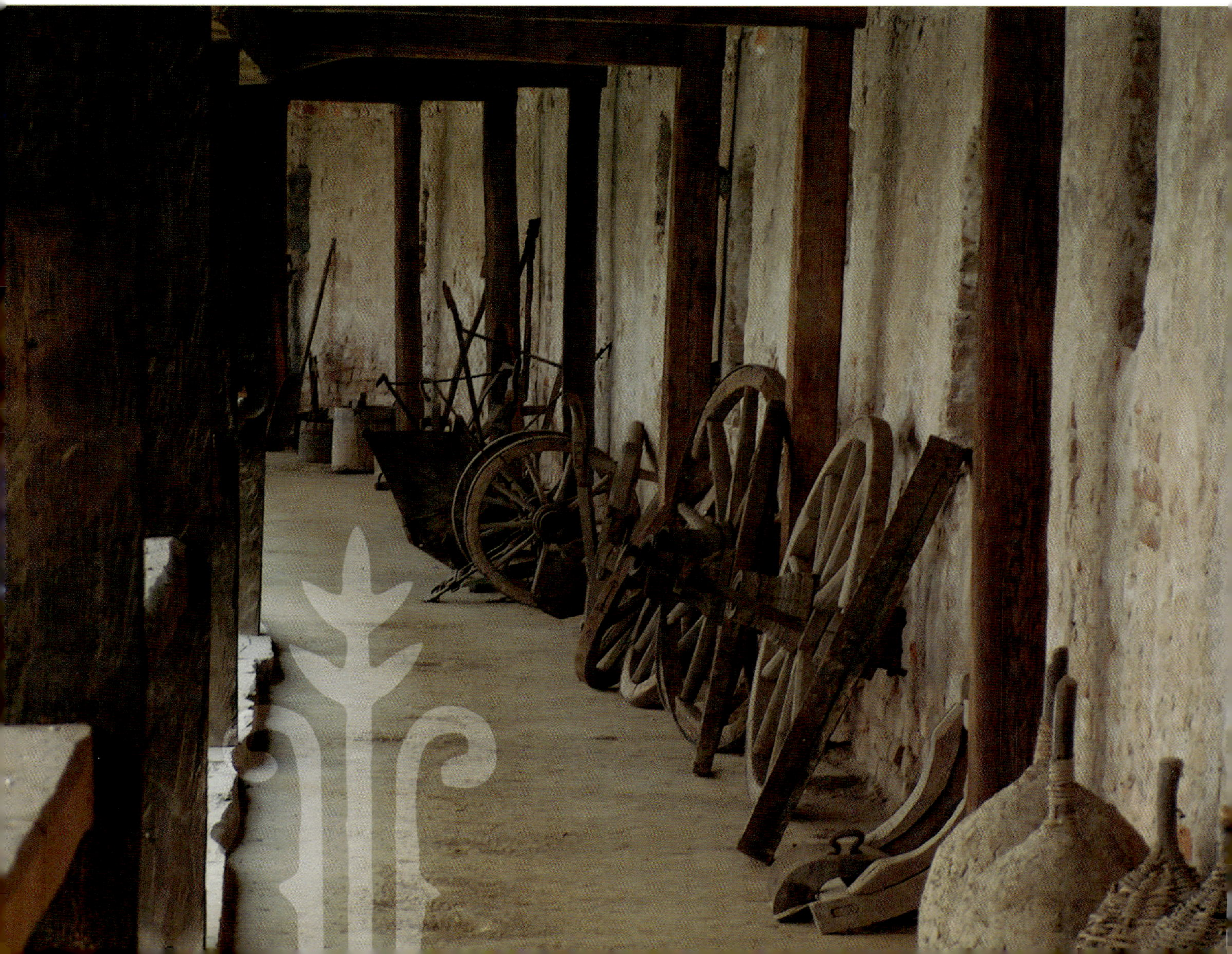

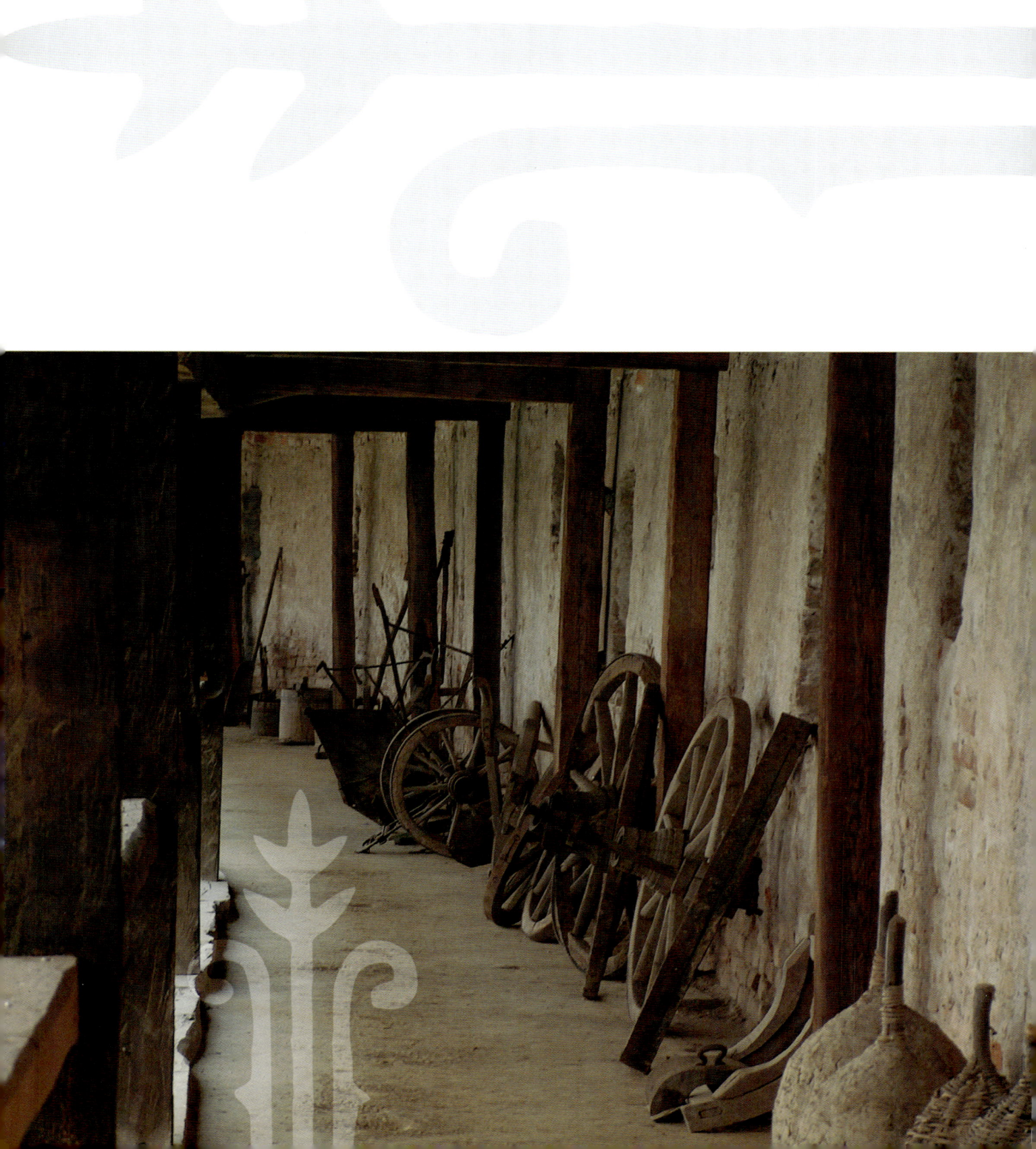

Moșna
Meschen

Brateiu
Pretai

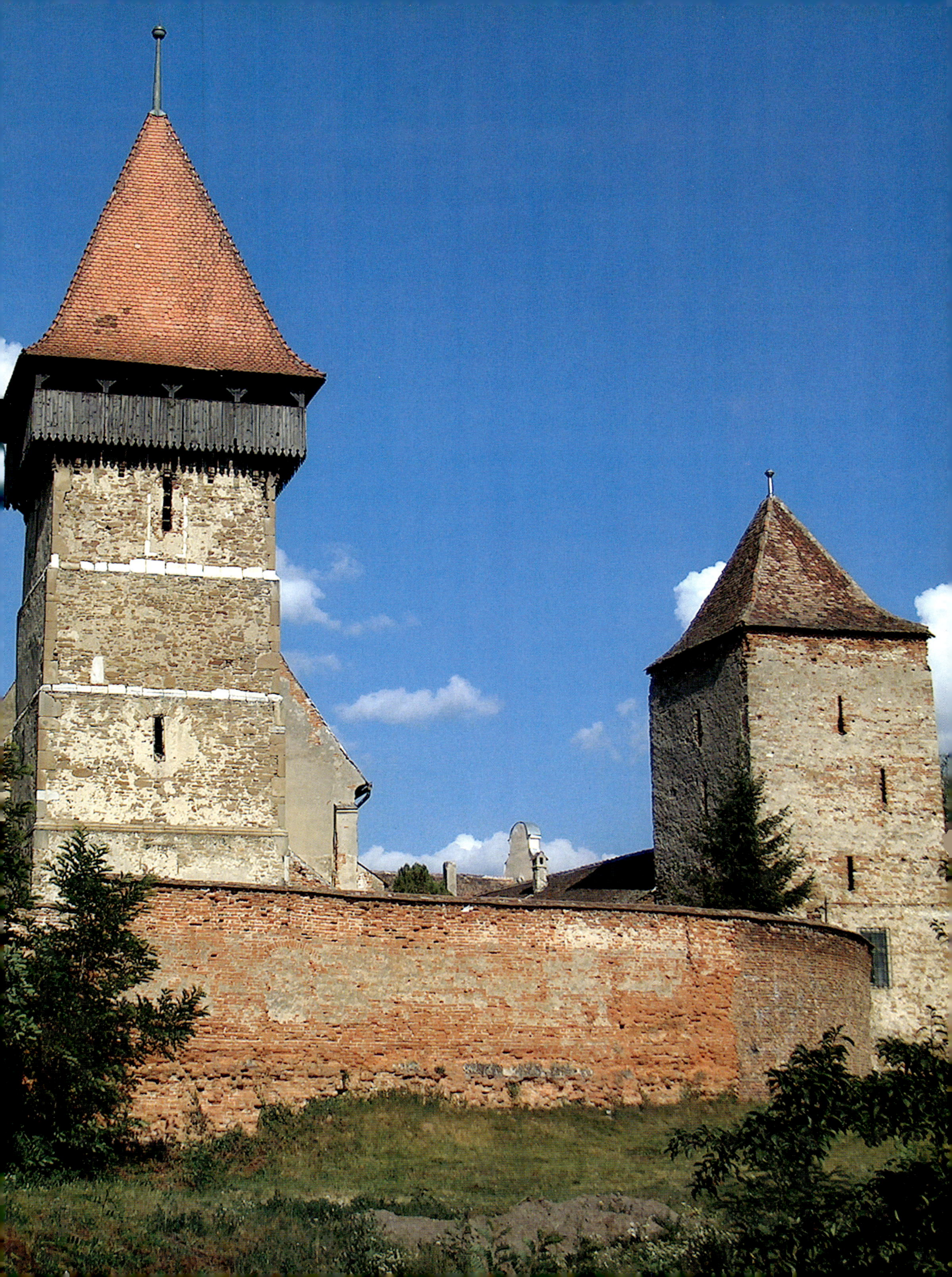

Dârlos
Durles

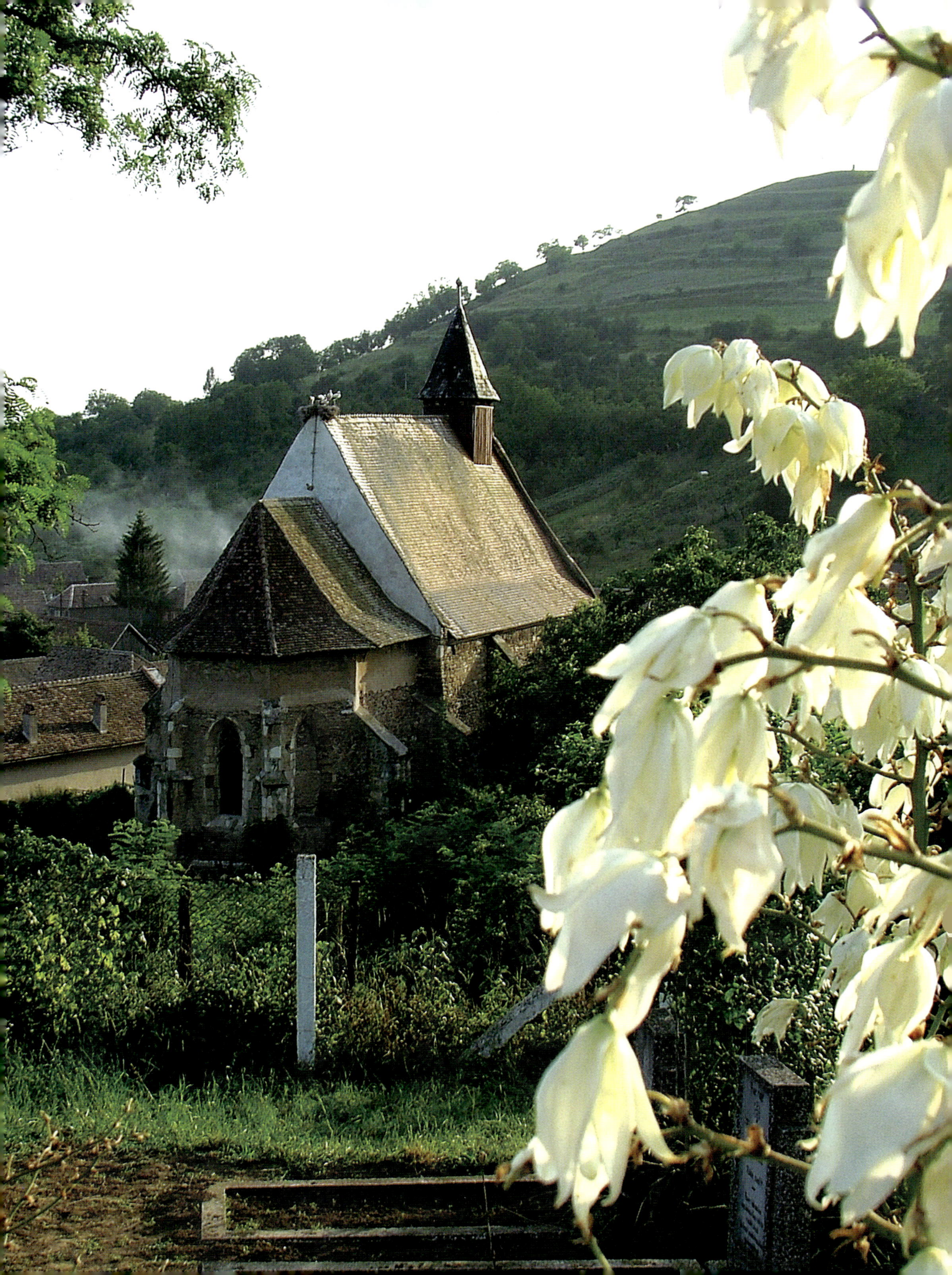

Curciu
Kirtsch

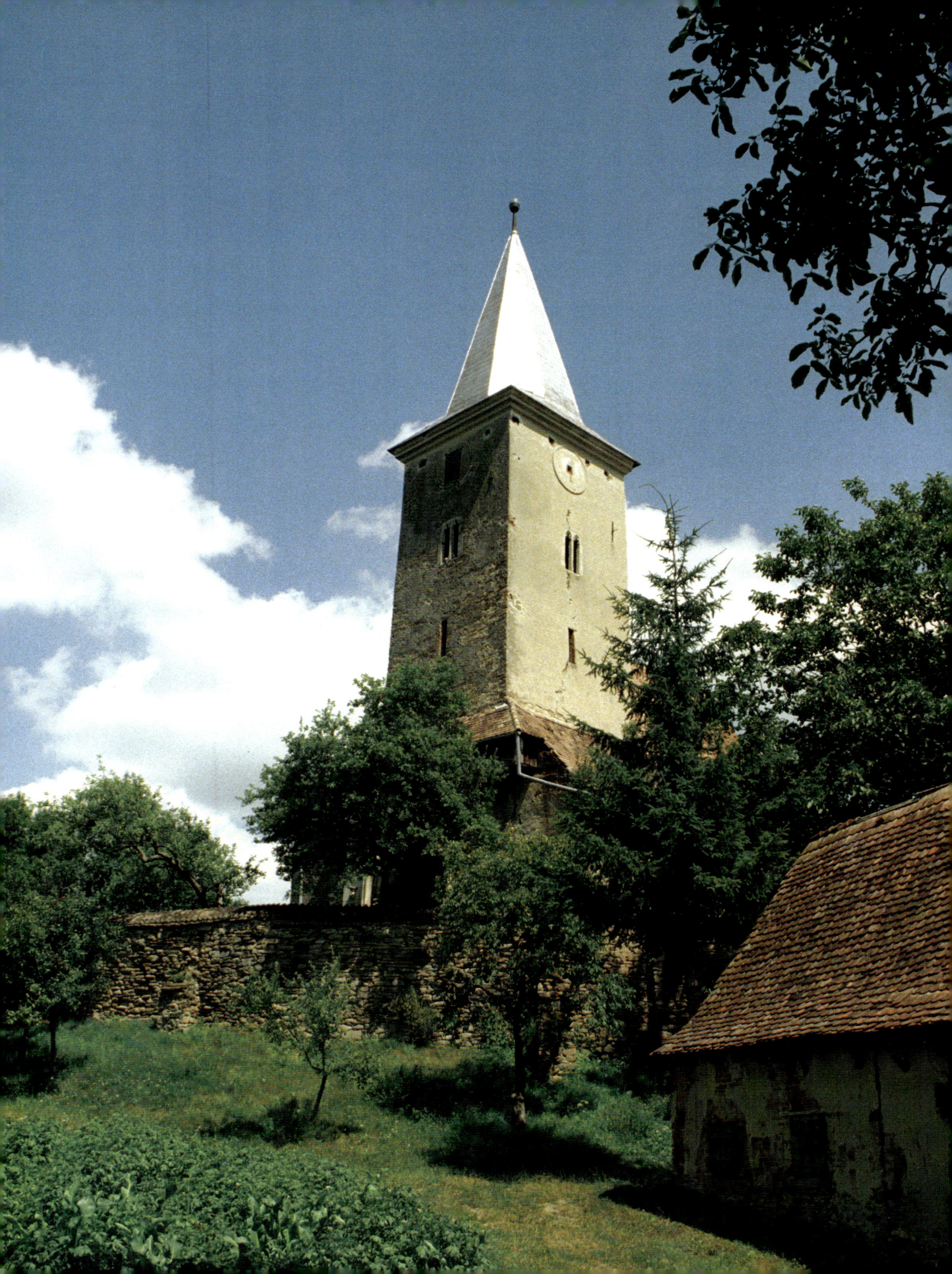

BĂGACIU

BOGESCHDORF

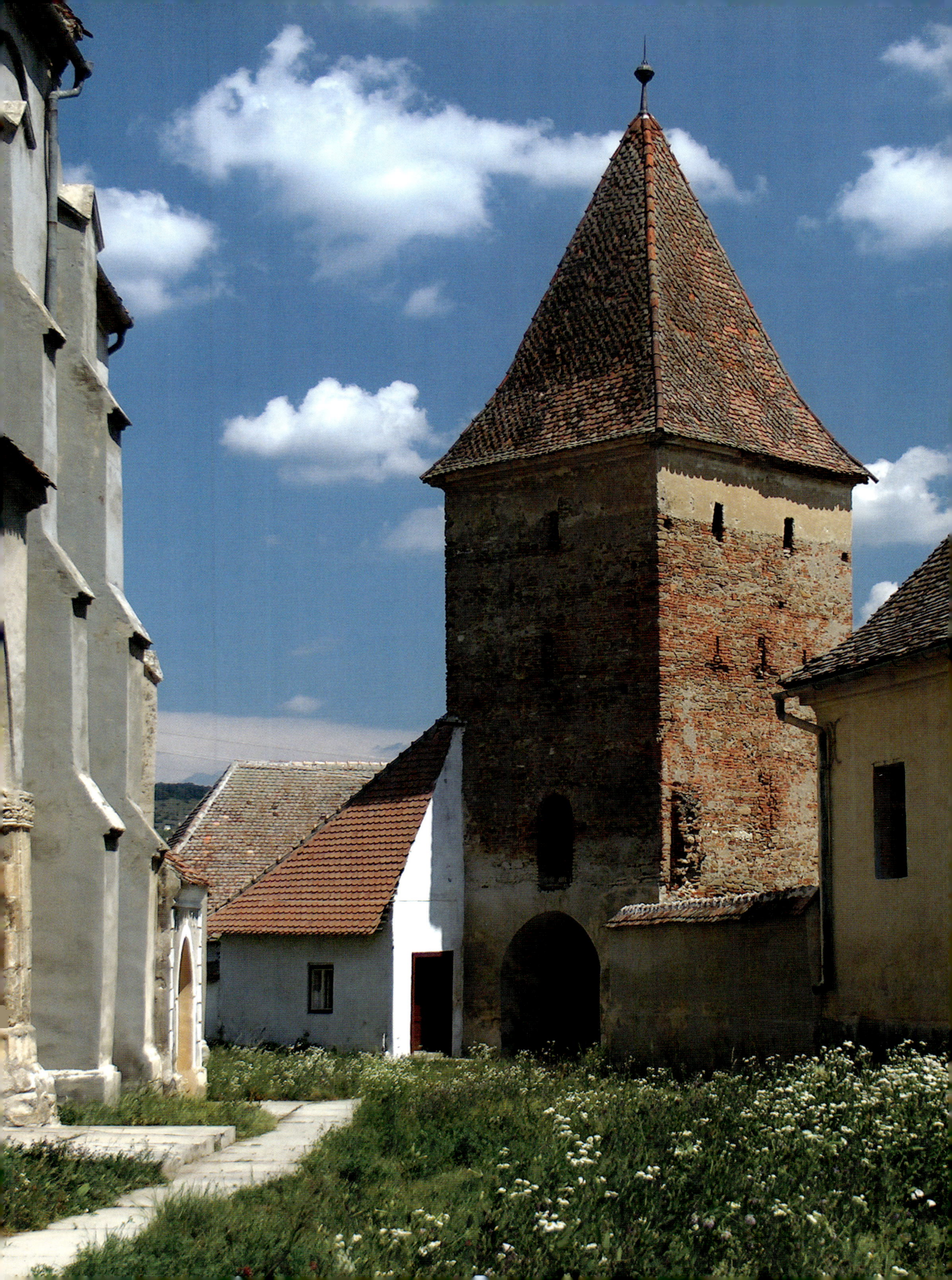

VELȚ

WÖLZ

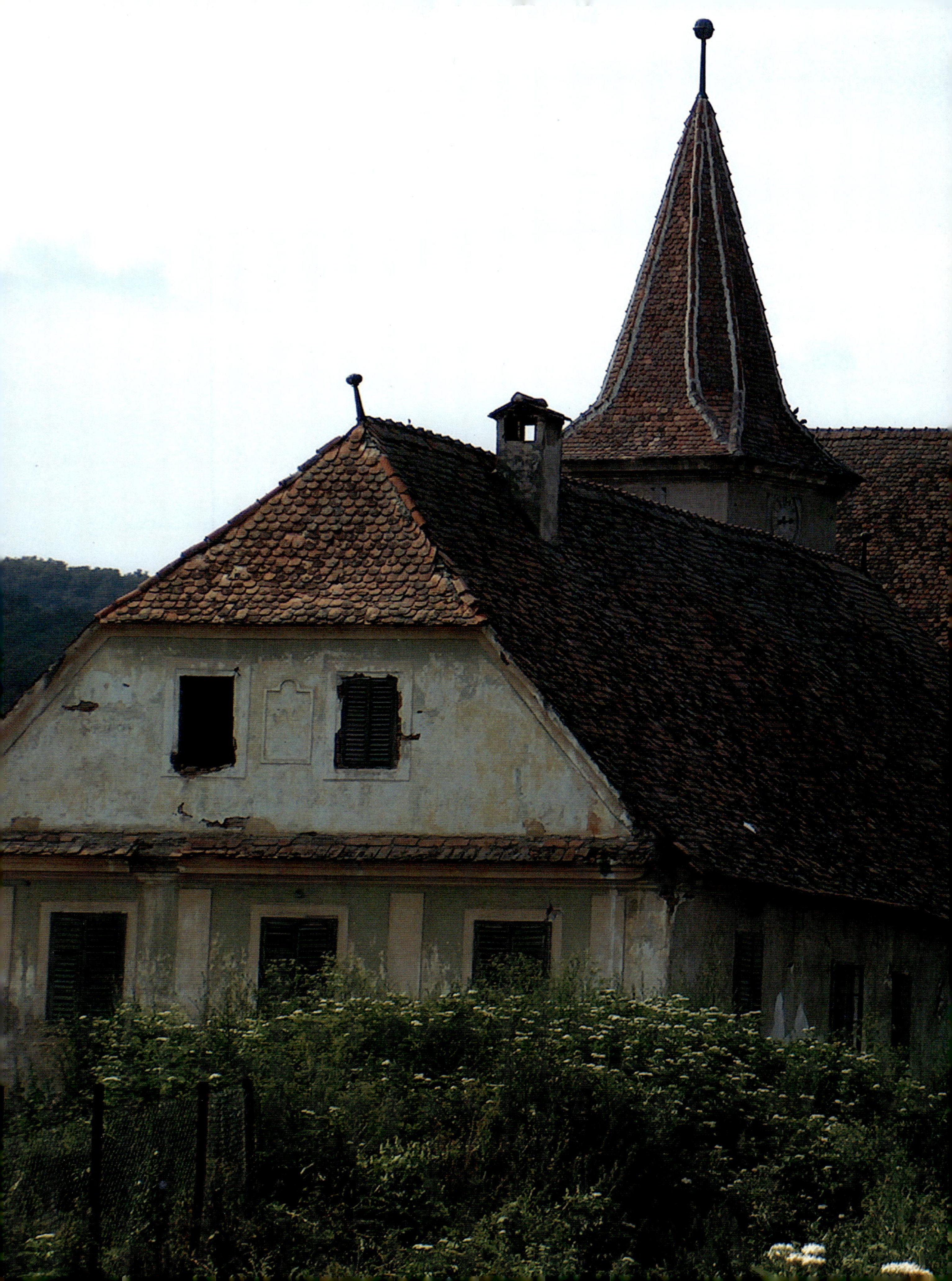

Bazna
Baaßen

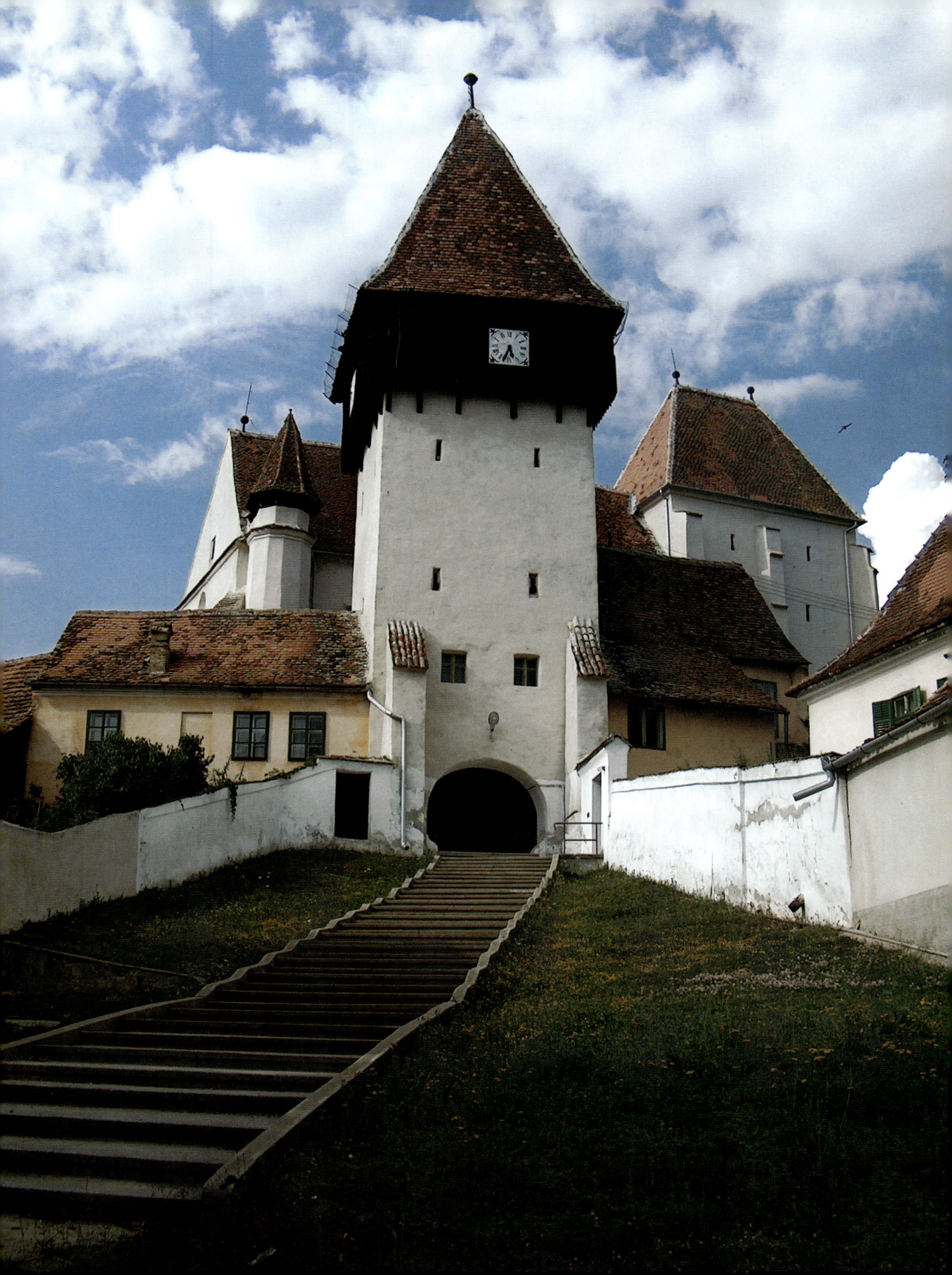

Mediaş
Mediasch

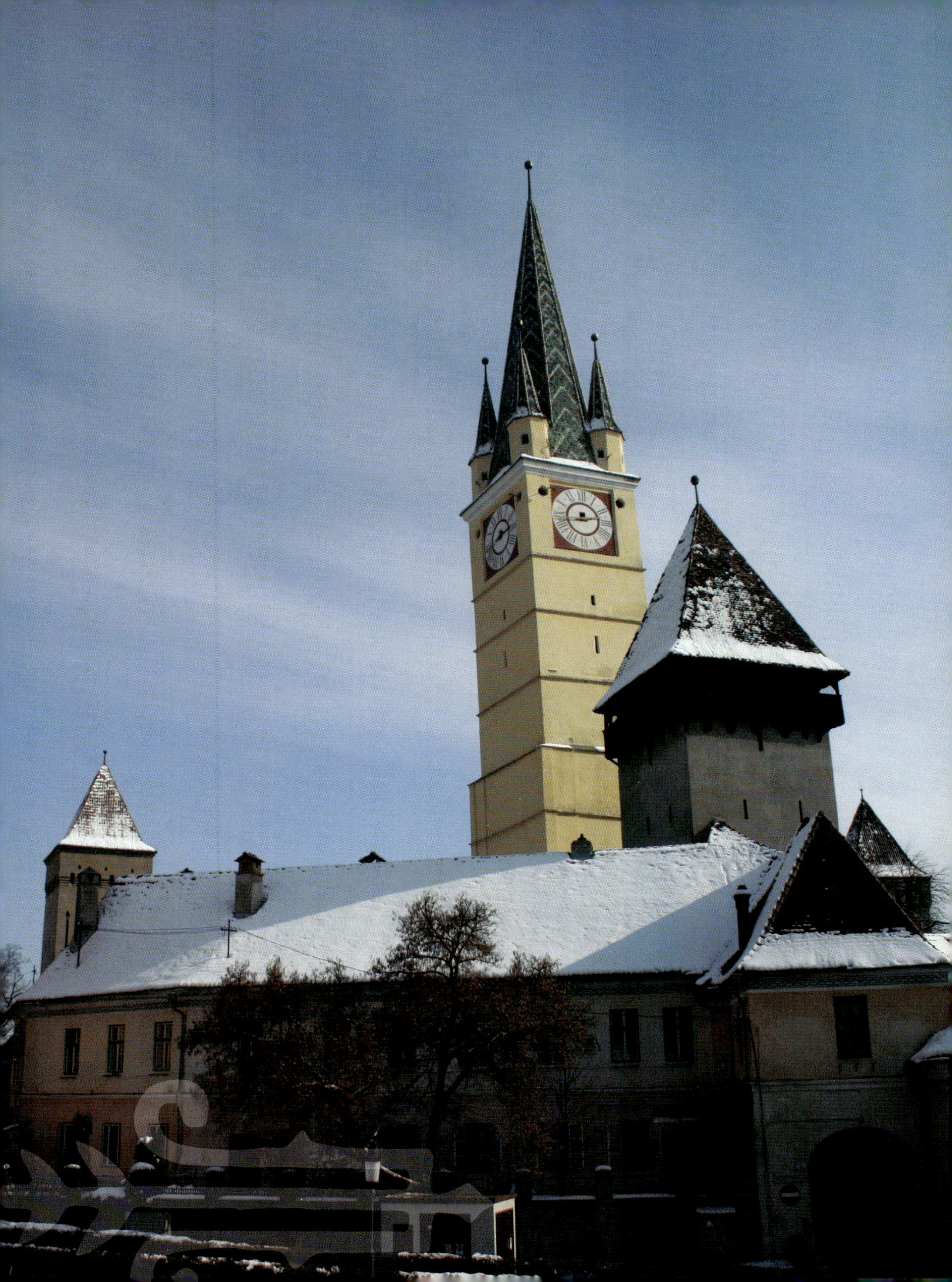

Valea Viilor
Wurmloch

WORLD HERITAGE

Ighișu Nou

Eibesdorf

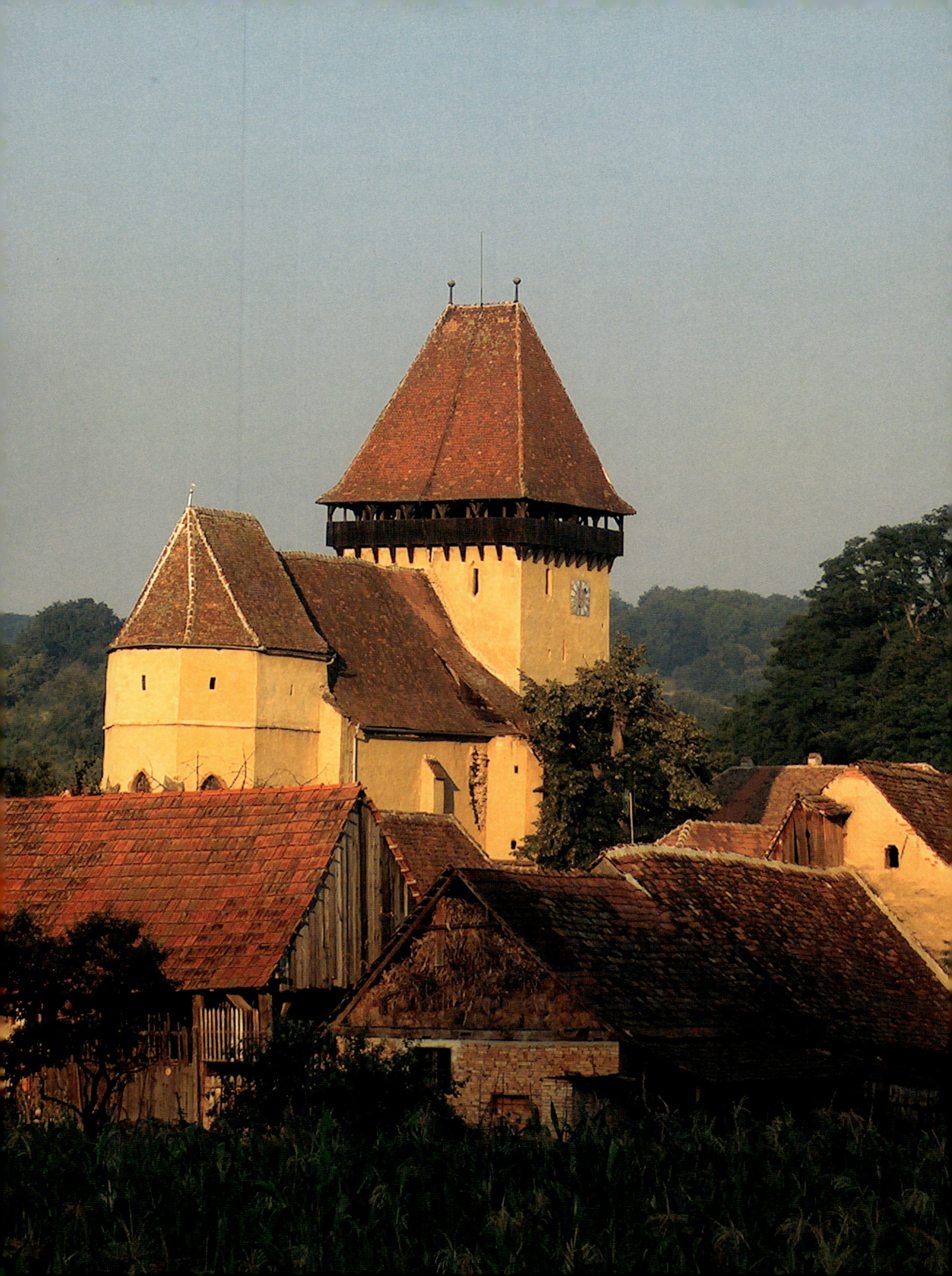

Axente Sever
Frauendorf

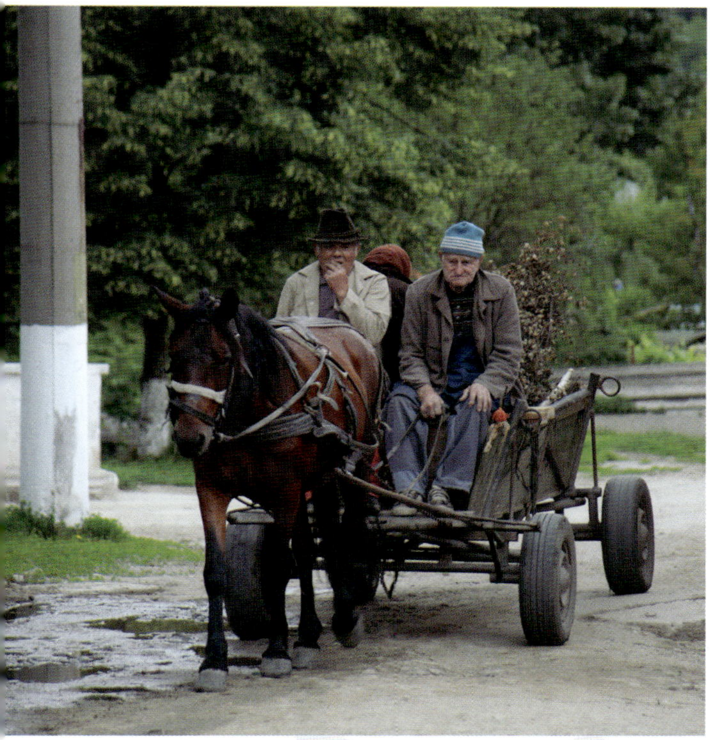
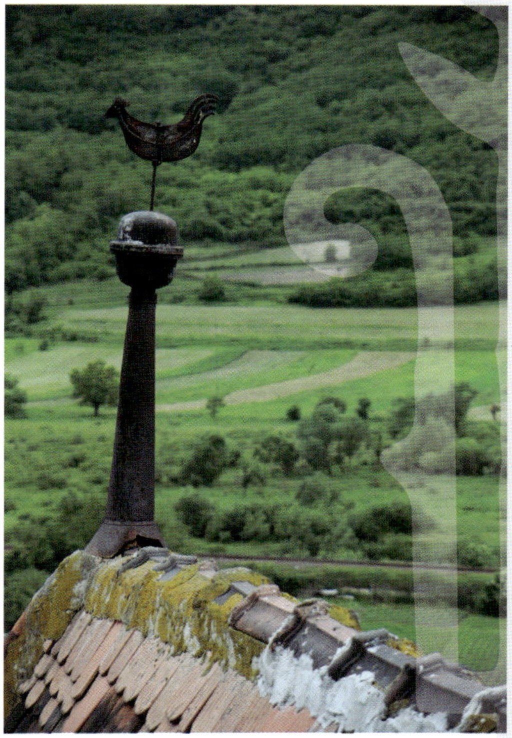
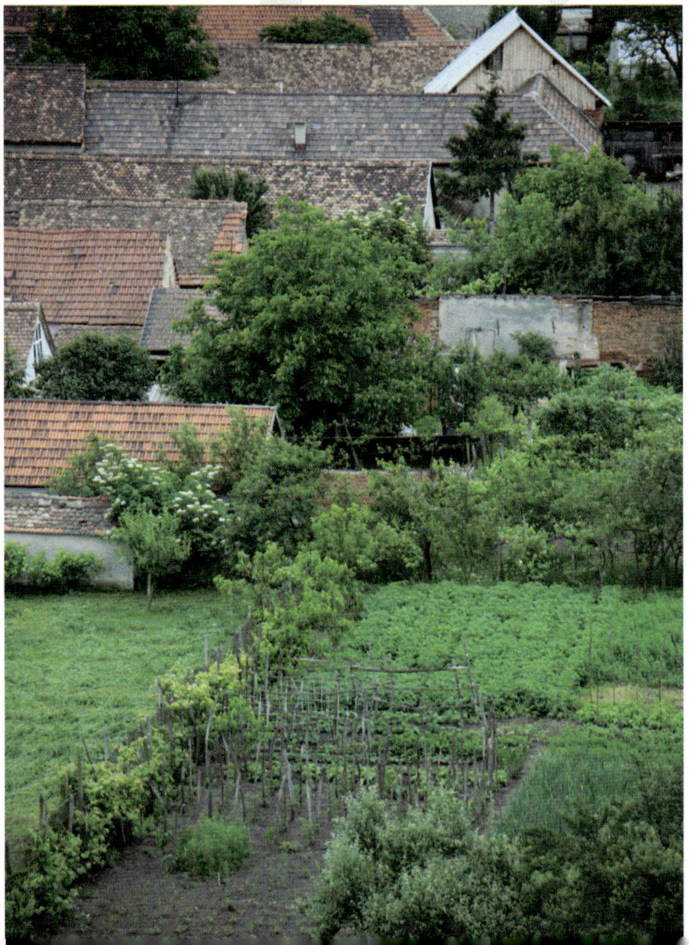
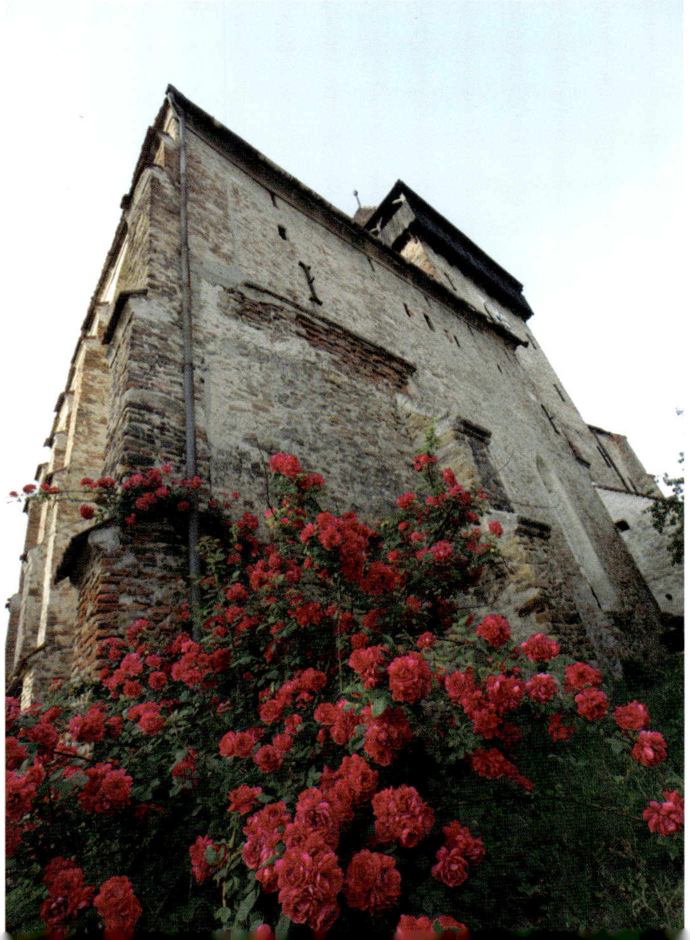

Hidden Treasures

Flames dance around over a treasure on the eve of certain holidays. It is said that evil little demons have a laugh tempting people and making them forget there is a holiday coming up.

Around this area, the word is that there are a lot of treasures. The first thing you see is a little dancing blue flame. Try to get close to it and it moves away. It seems so close, yet it always is one step away from reach. Sometimes, while running around after dancing flames, at a street corner or by a bridge, you may run into a little man with a red cap and a pipe. He just sits there and looks at you and you would almost want to greet him. But in the blink of an eye he vanishes. This a bad omen, and you should walk away, for peculiar accidents in those whereabouts. But the flame keeps dancing and calling for you. Legends tell of many a man who lost their way in search of flames.

Somewhere in the area of Aţel, on Treasure Hill, two golden ploughs are said to have been buried inside a cave. Alas the entrance of the cave only opens once a year and only for an hour. Nobody has found it yet, or maybe they just didn't live to tell the tale.

Versteckte Schätze

In dieser Gegend sind allerlei Schätze versteckt. So heißt es zumindest. Erst hat man den Eindruck, ein flackerndes blaues Lichtlein zu sehen. Je näher man ihm geht, desto weiter zieht es sich zurück. Es scheint so nahe und ist es doch nicht. Manchmal kann es passieren, dass man, während man dem Flämmchen nachläuft, an einer Wegbiegung oder auf einer Brücke ein Männlein mit roter Mütze und einer Pfeife im Mund antrifft. Der steht da und sieht einen an, als erwarte er einen Gruß. Sieht man aber ein zweites Mal hin, ist er verschwunden. Das ist ein Zeichen, dass dieses ein verwunschener Ort ist, und den sollte man so schnell wie möglich verlassen, denn da passieren gerne Unfälle. Das Flämmchen jedoch flackert weiter, ruft einen. Es gibt eine Menge Erzählungen über Menschen, die sich verirrt haben, da sie dem Flämmchen nachgelaufen sind.

Die Flammen sieht man da, wo Schätze vergraben sind, doch nur am Vorabend gewisser Feiertage, so, als ob der Teufel beabsichtigen würde, dem Betreffenden den Verstand zu verdunkeln, damit der vergisst, dass ein Feiertag kommt.

Irgendwo neben Hetzeldorf (Atel), beim "Schatzberg", gibt es - so sagt man - eine Höhle, in der zwei goldene Pflüge vergraben sind. Doch der Eingang zu dieser Höhle öffnet sich nur einmal im Jahr und nur für eine Stunde. Noch hat niemand diesen Eingang gefunden. Oder vielleicht, wer weiß, konnte er nicht mehr herauskommen.

Sibiu - Agnita

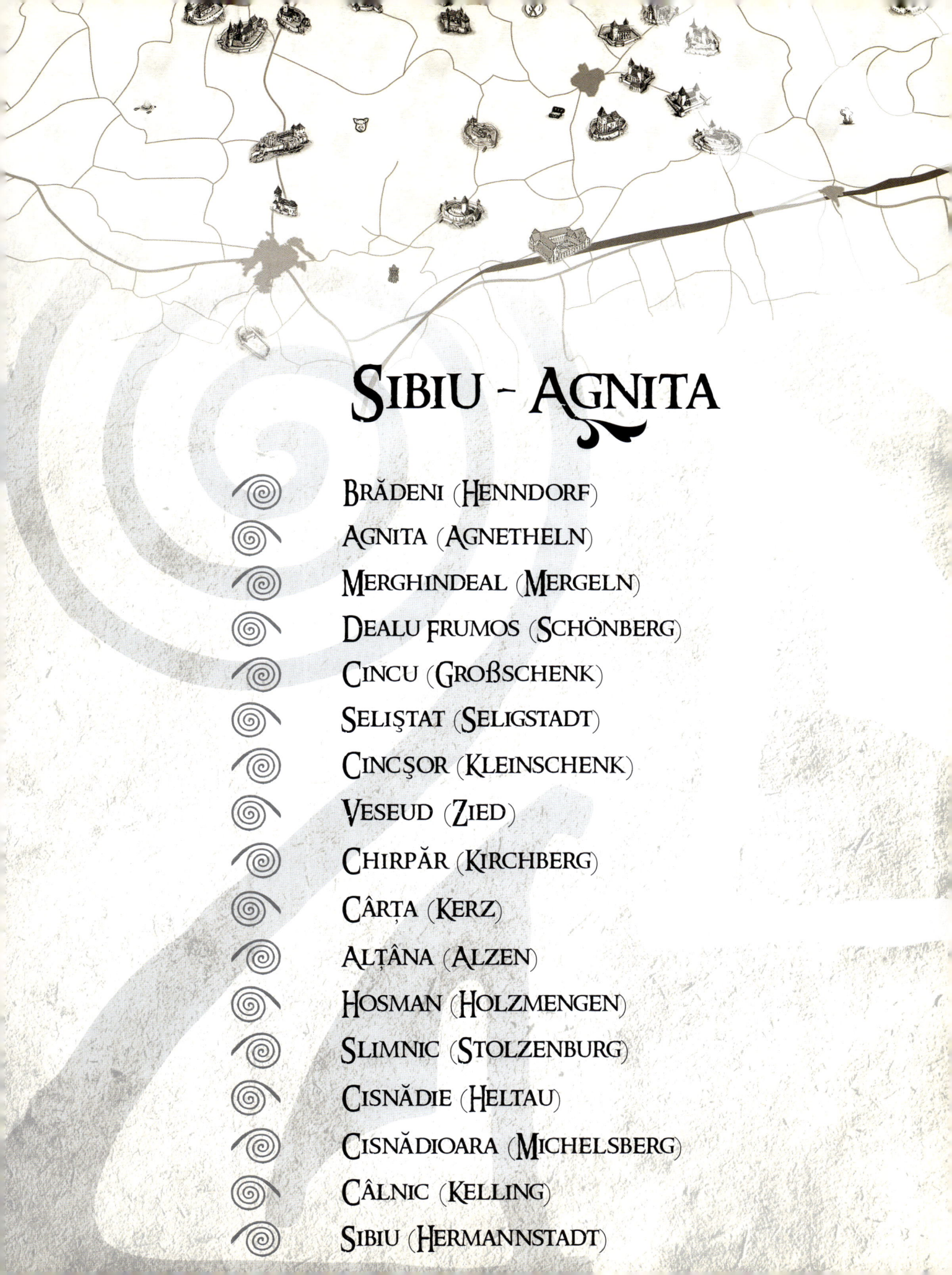

- Brădeni (Henndorf)
- Agnita (Agnetheln)
- Merghindeal (Mergeln)
- Dealu Frumos (Schönberg)
- Cincu (Großschenk)
- Seliștat (Seligstadt)
- Cincșor (Kleinschenk)
- Veseud (Zied)
- Chirpăr (Kirchberg)
- Cârța (Kerz)
- Altâna (Alzen)
- Hosman (Holzmengen)
- Slimnic (Stolzenburg)
- Cisnădie (Heltau)
- Cisnădioara (Michelsberg)
- Câlnic (Kelling)
- Sibiu (Hermannstadt)

BRĂDENI

HENNDORF

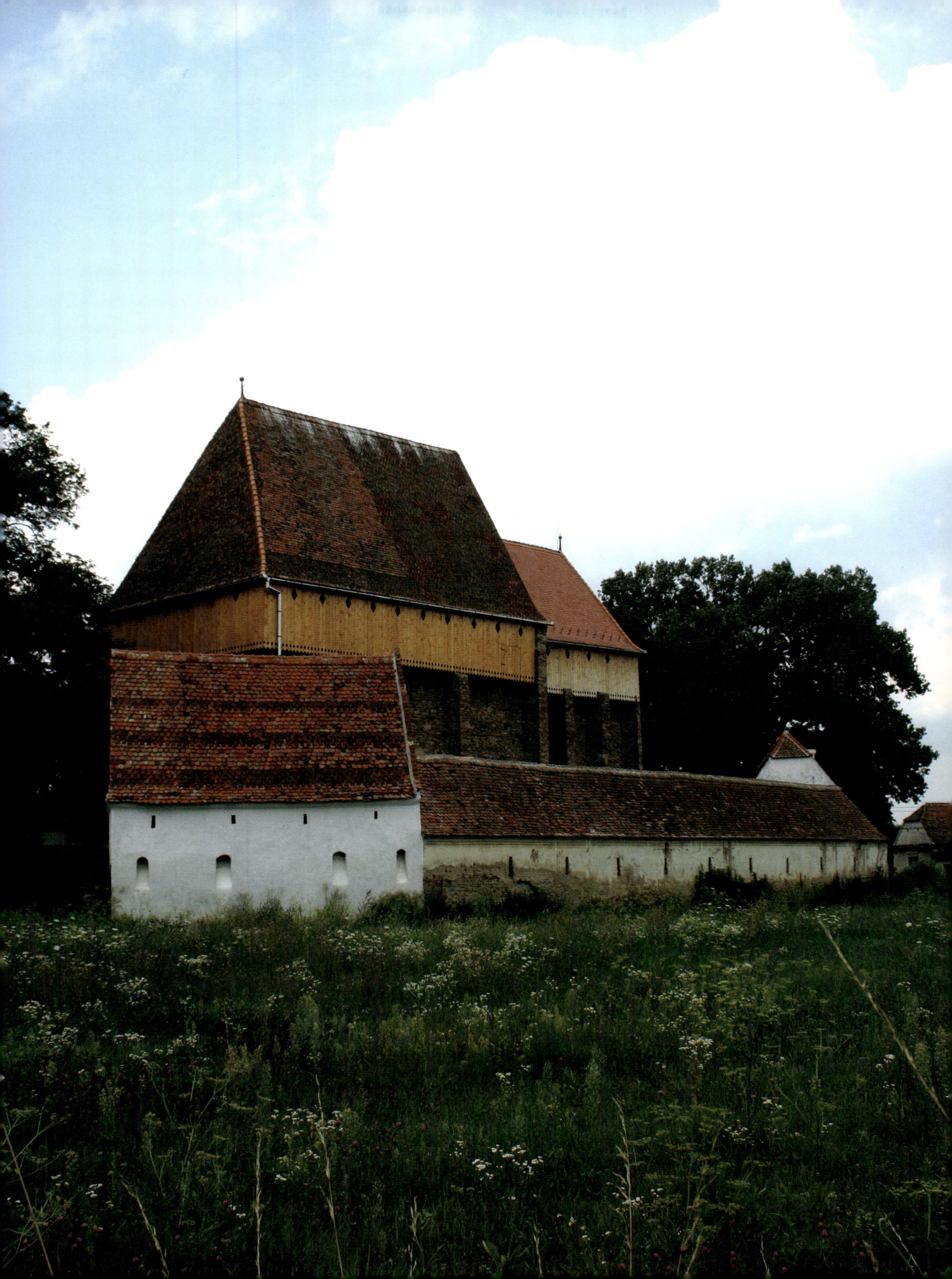

Agnita
Agnetheln

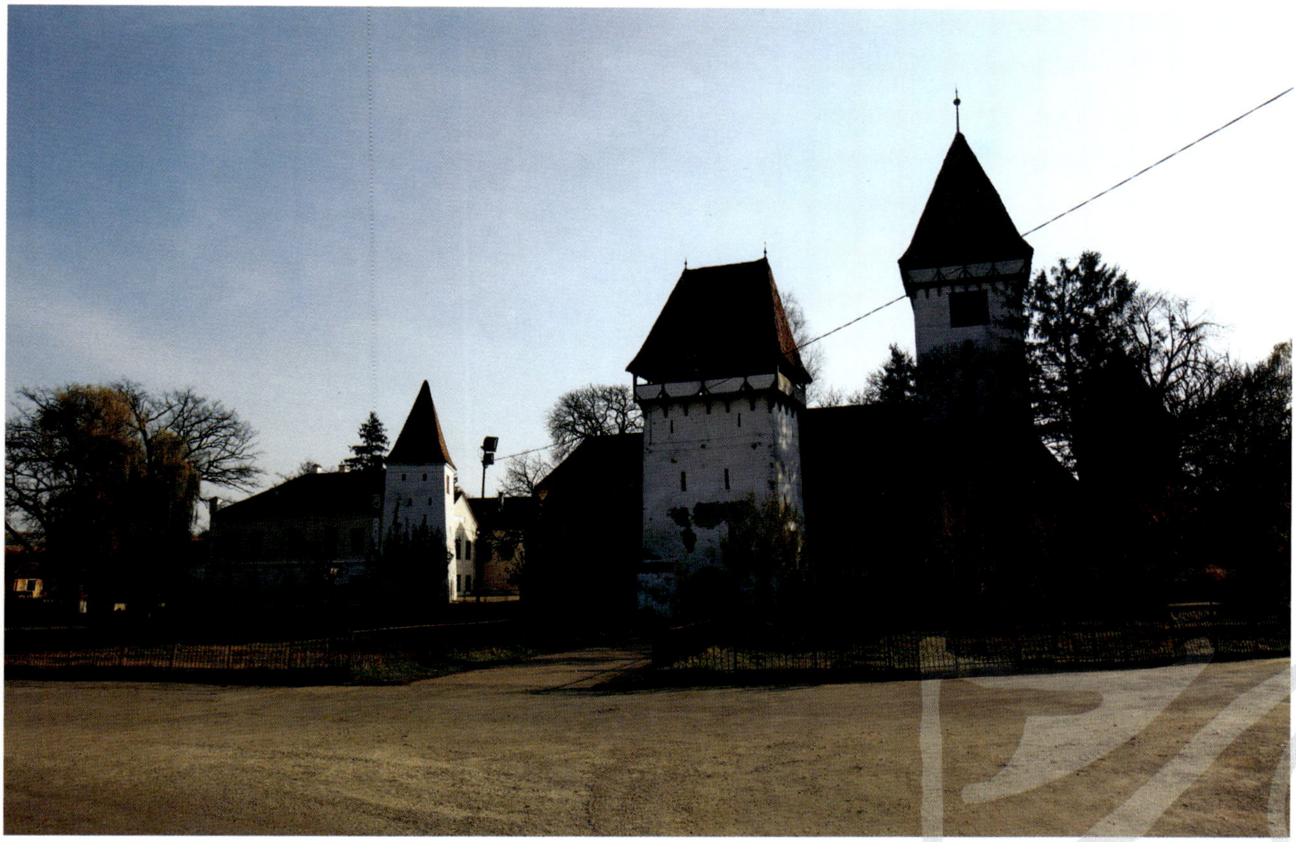

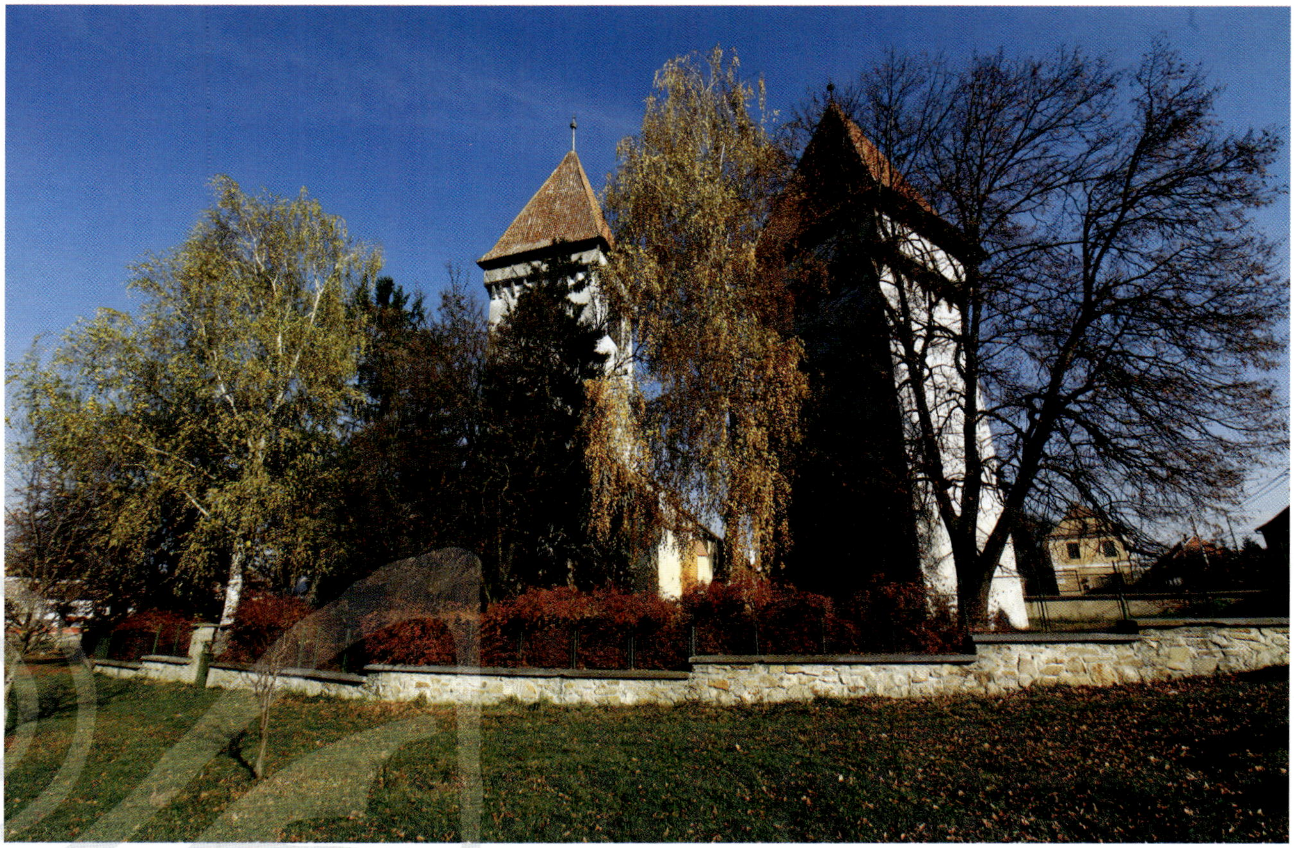

Merghindeal
Mergeln

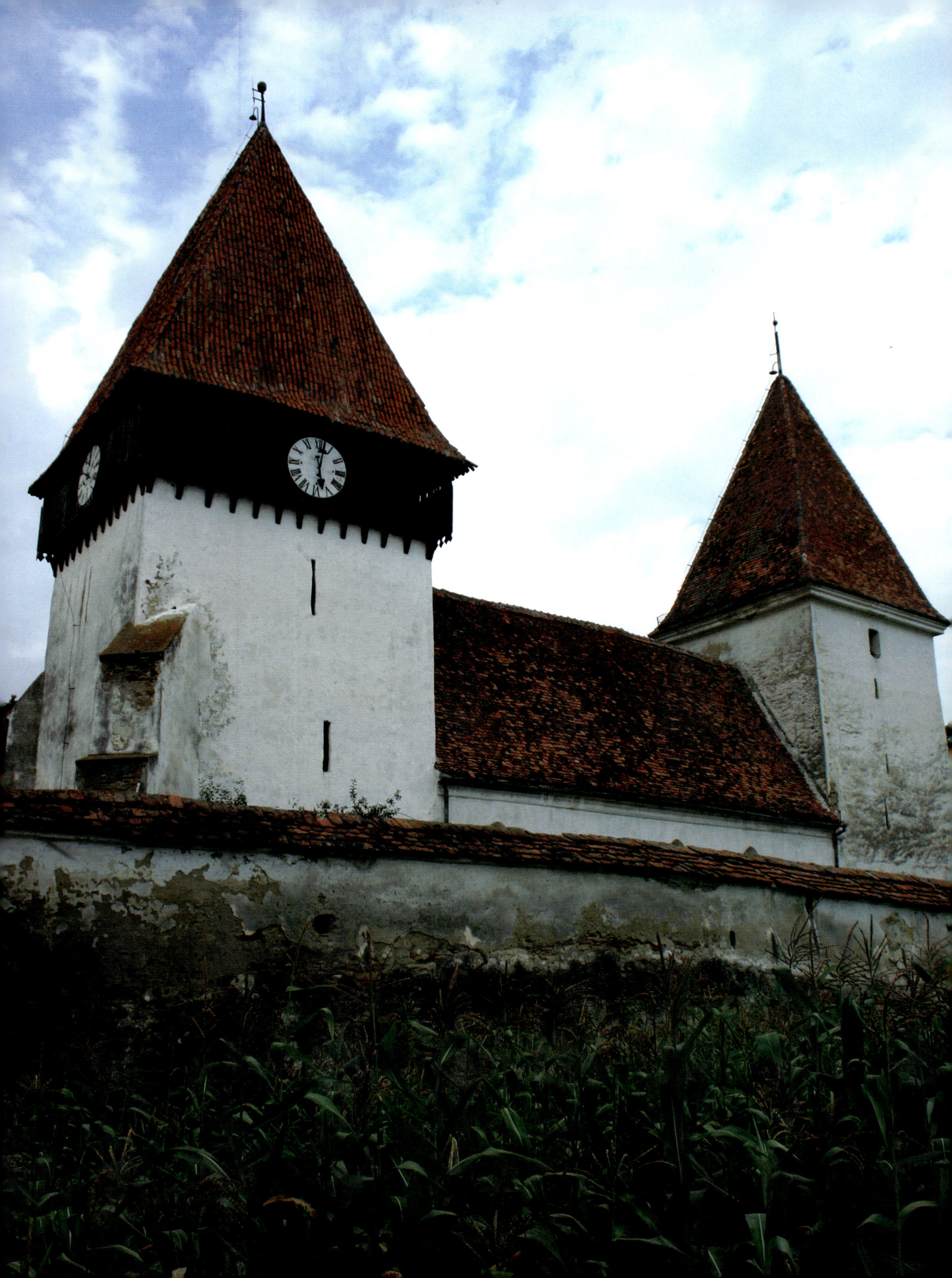

Dealu Frumos
Schönberg

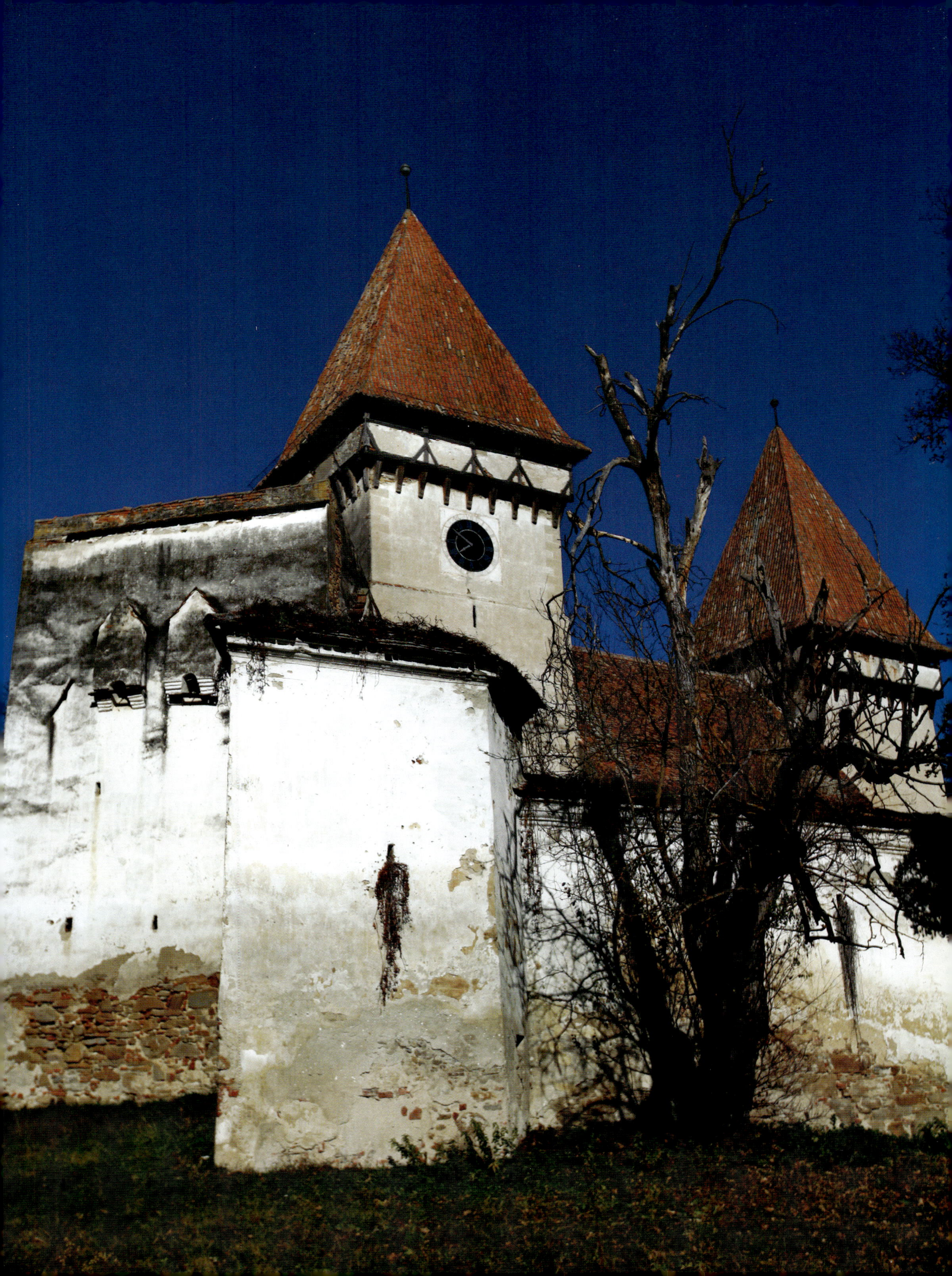

Cincu

Großschenk

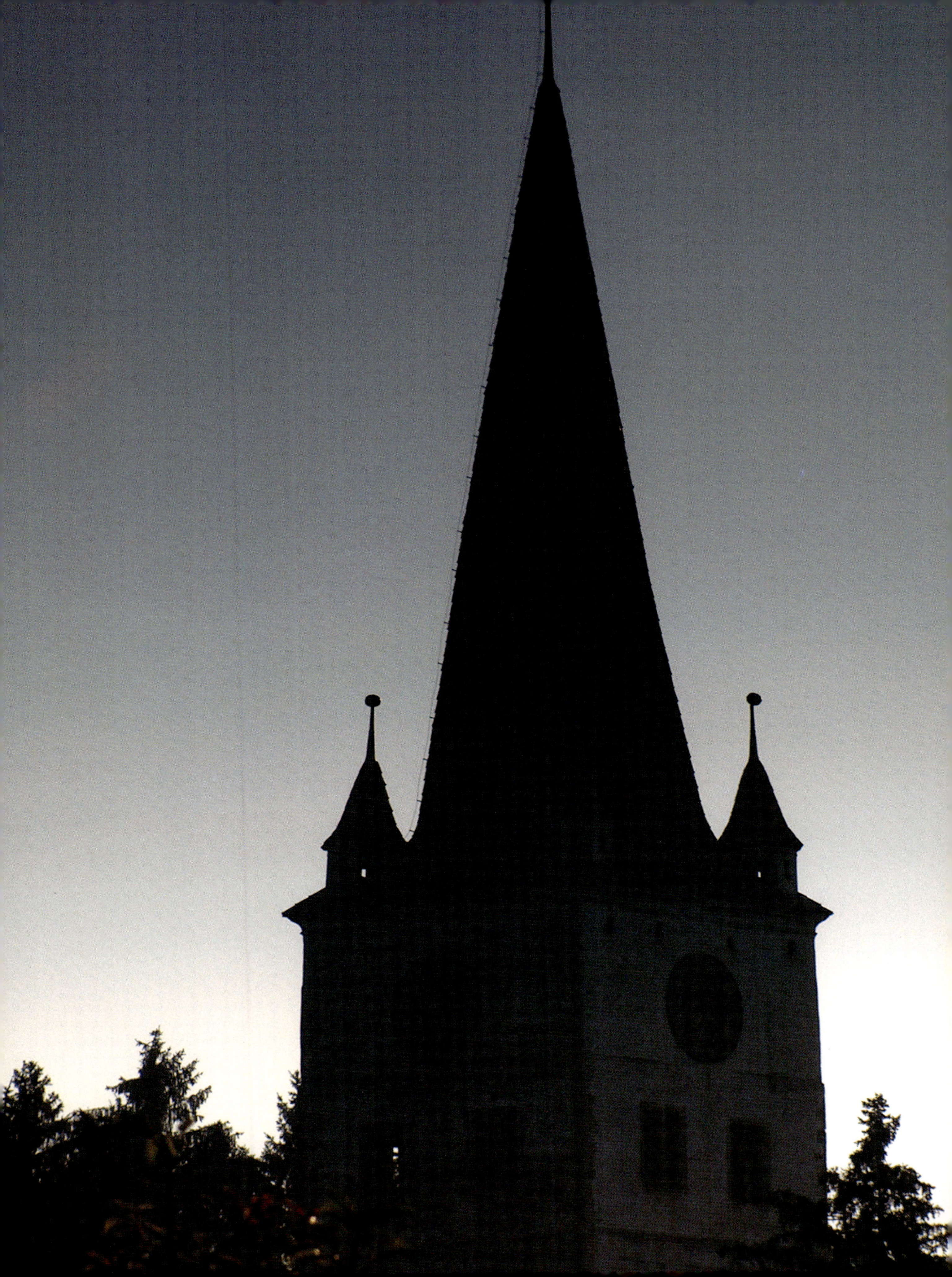

Seliștat
Seligstadt

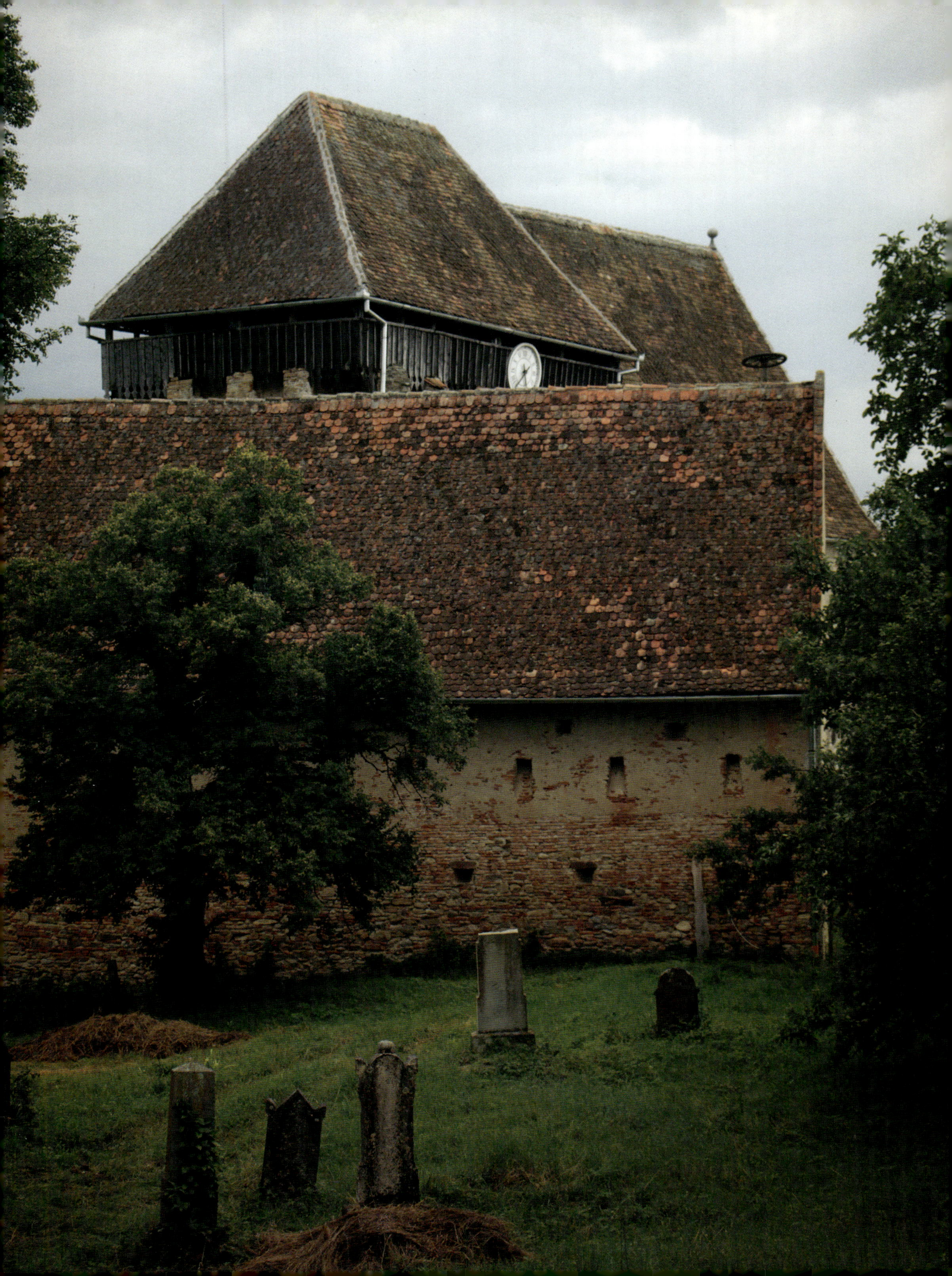

Cincșor
Kleinschenk

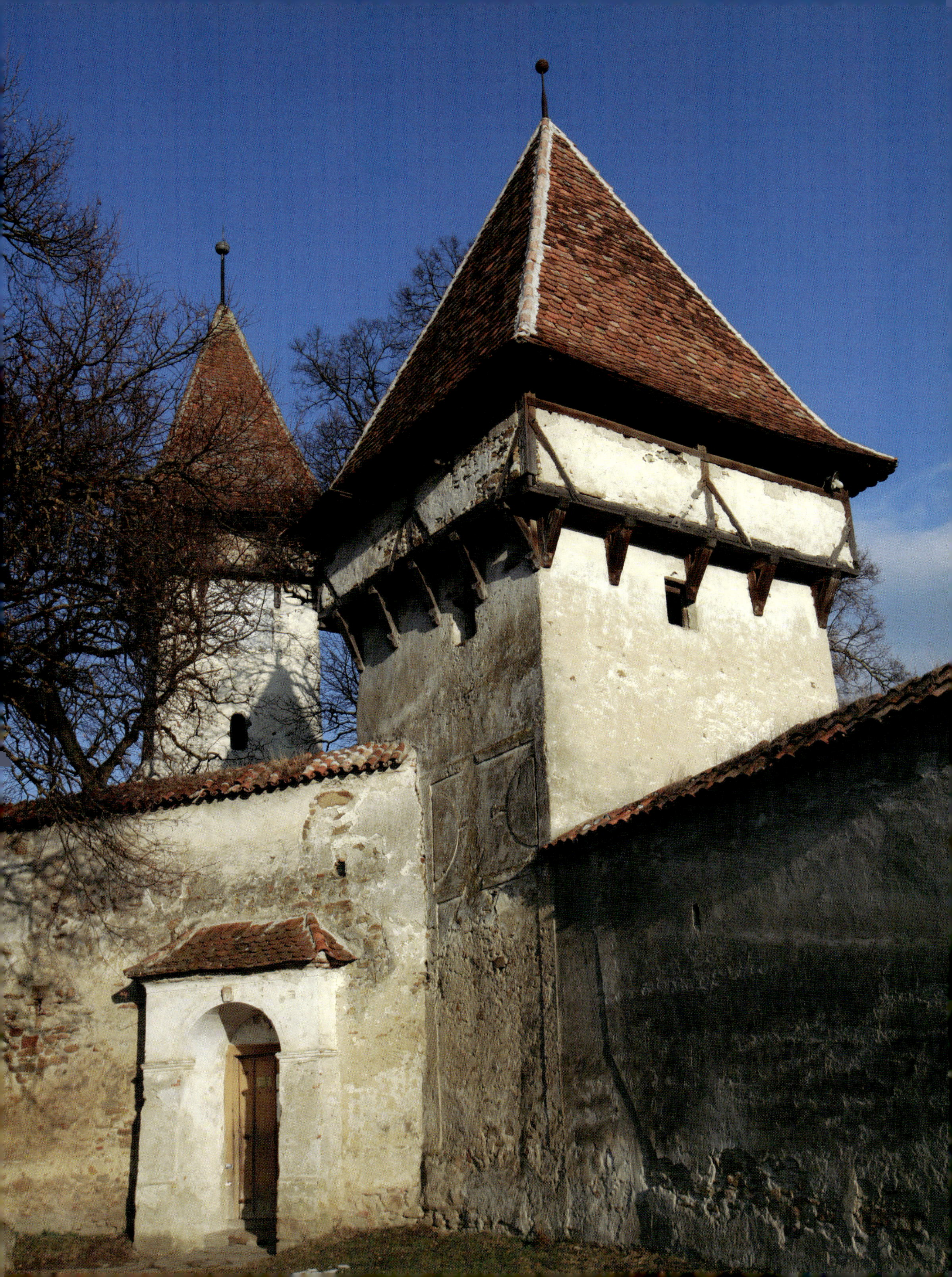

Veseud

Zied

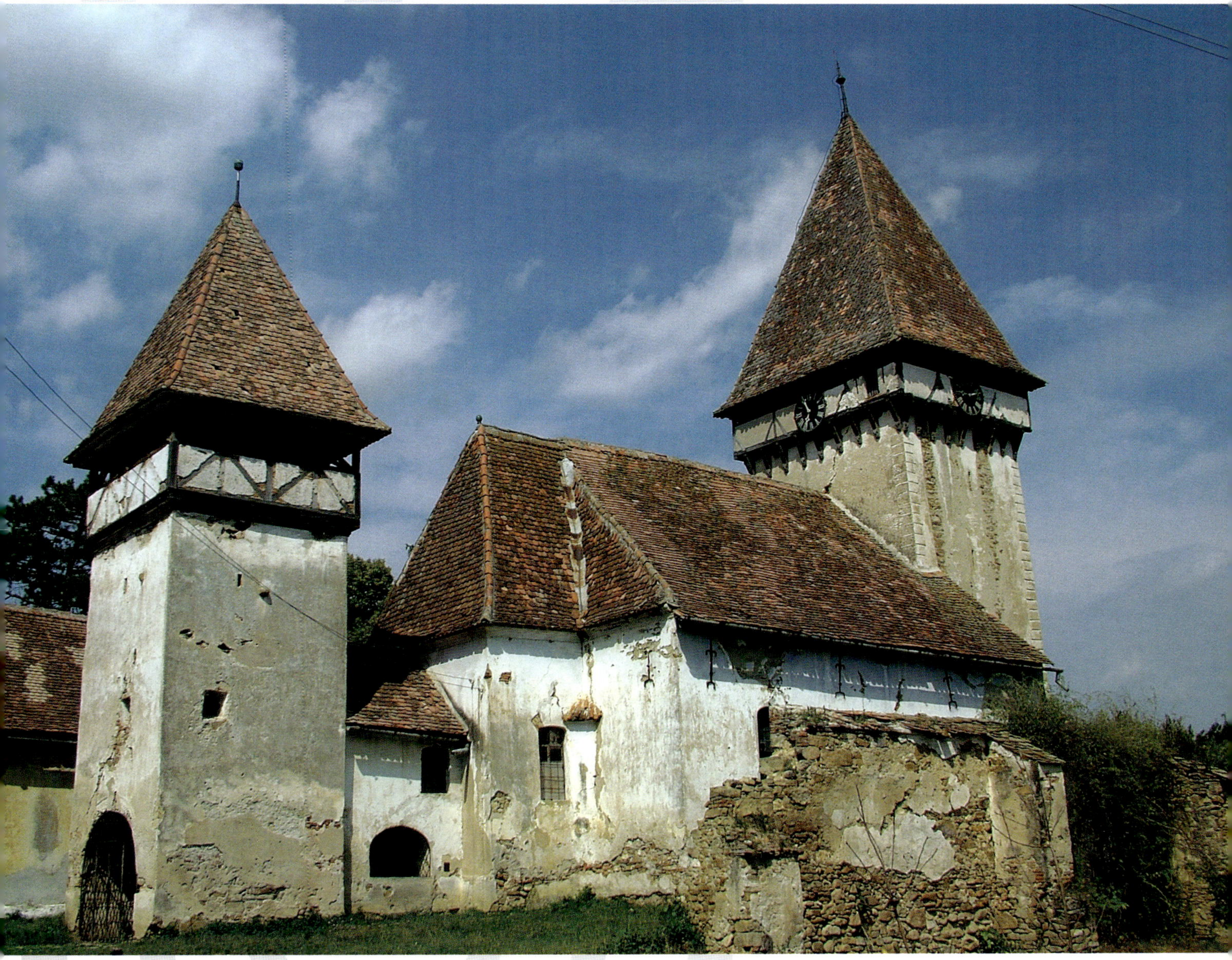

Chirpăr
Kirchberg

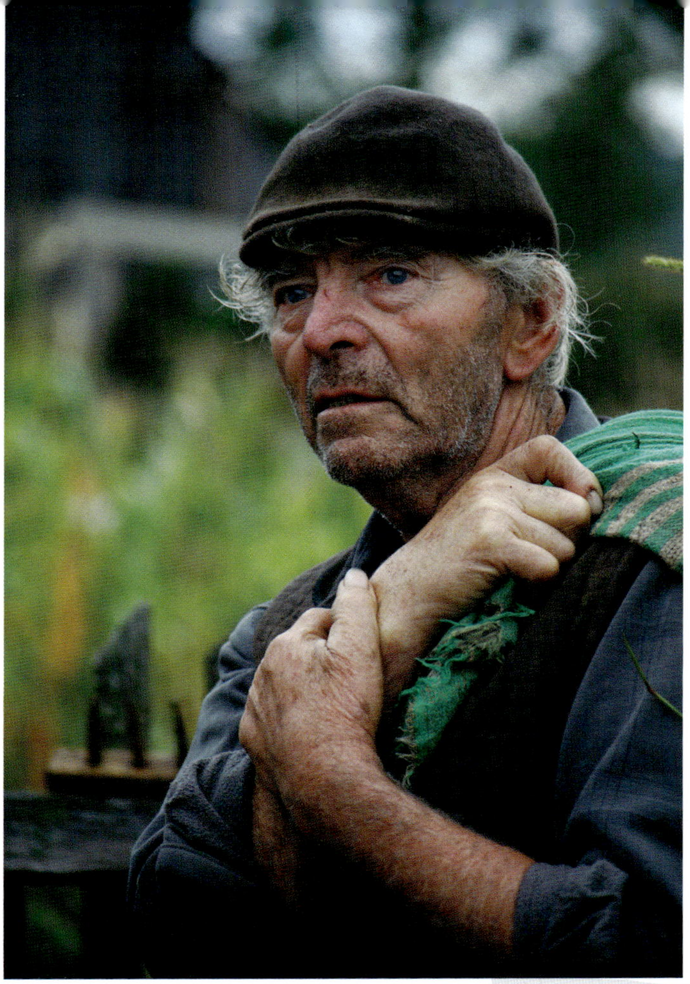
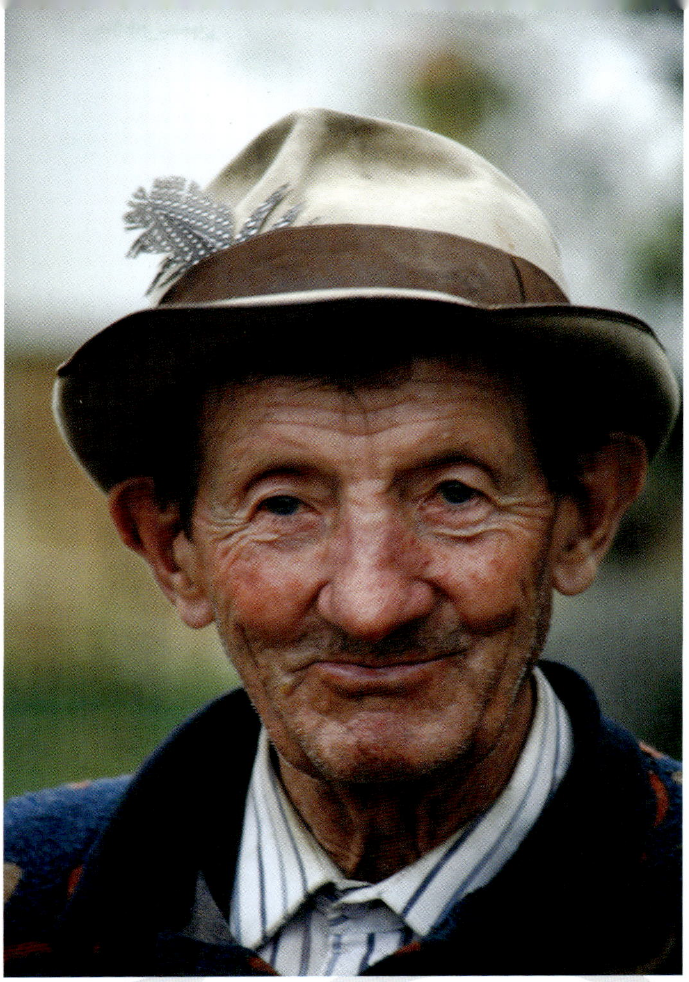
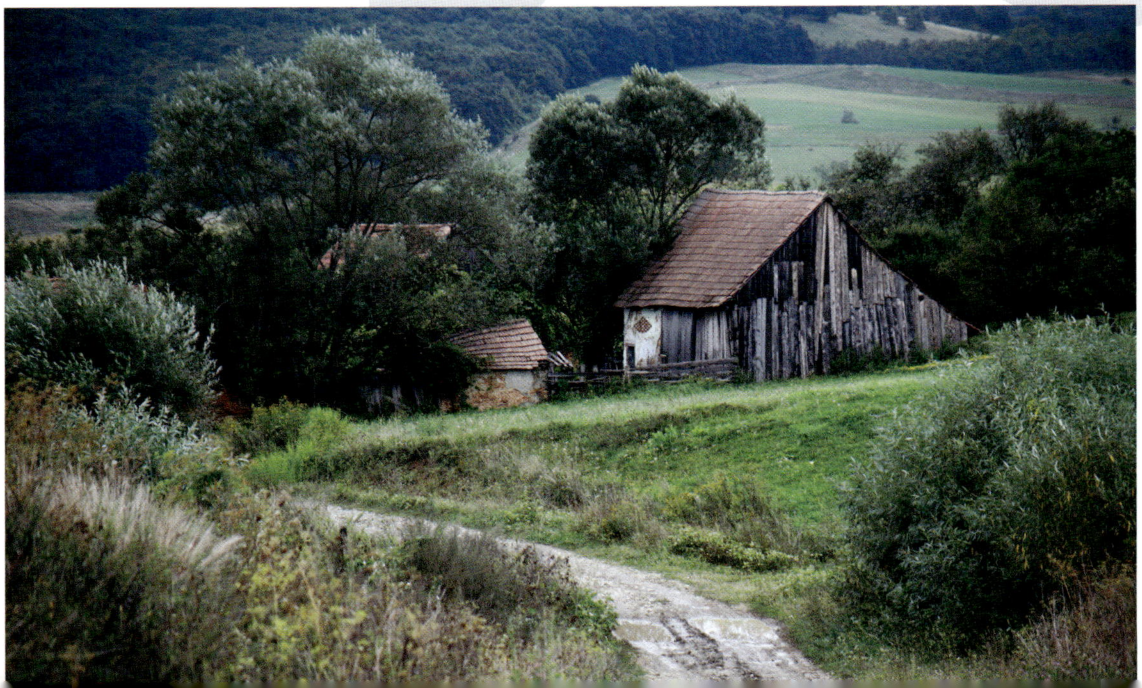

Cârța
Kerz

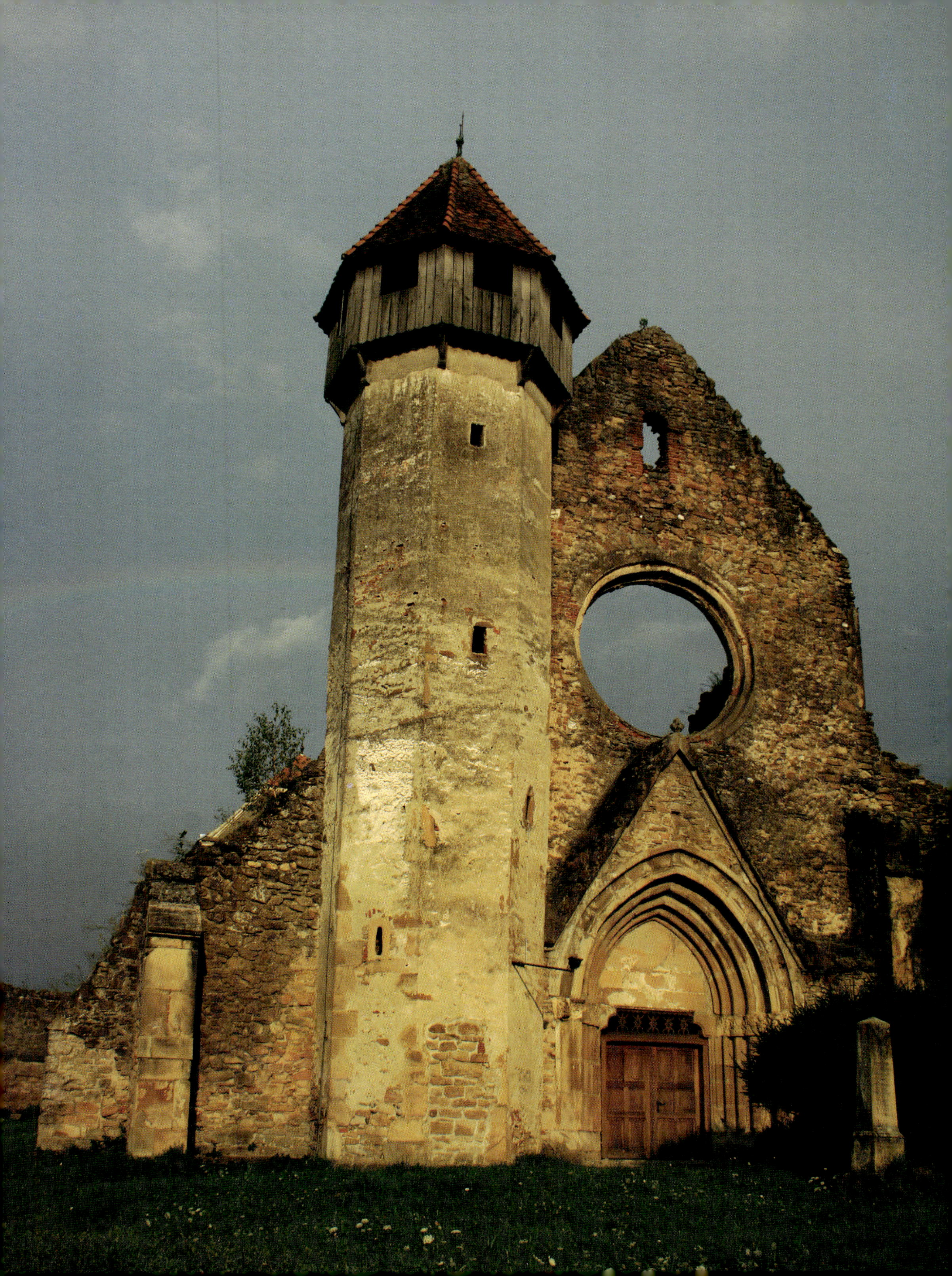

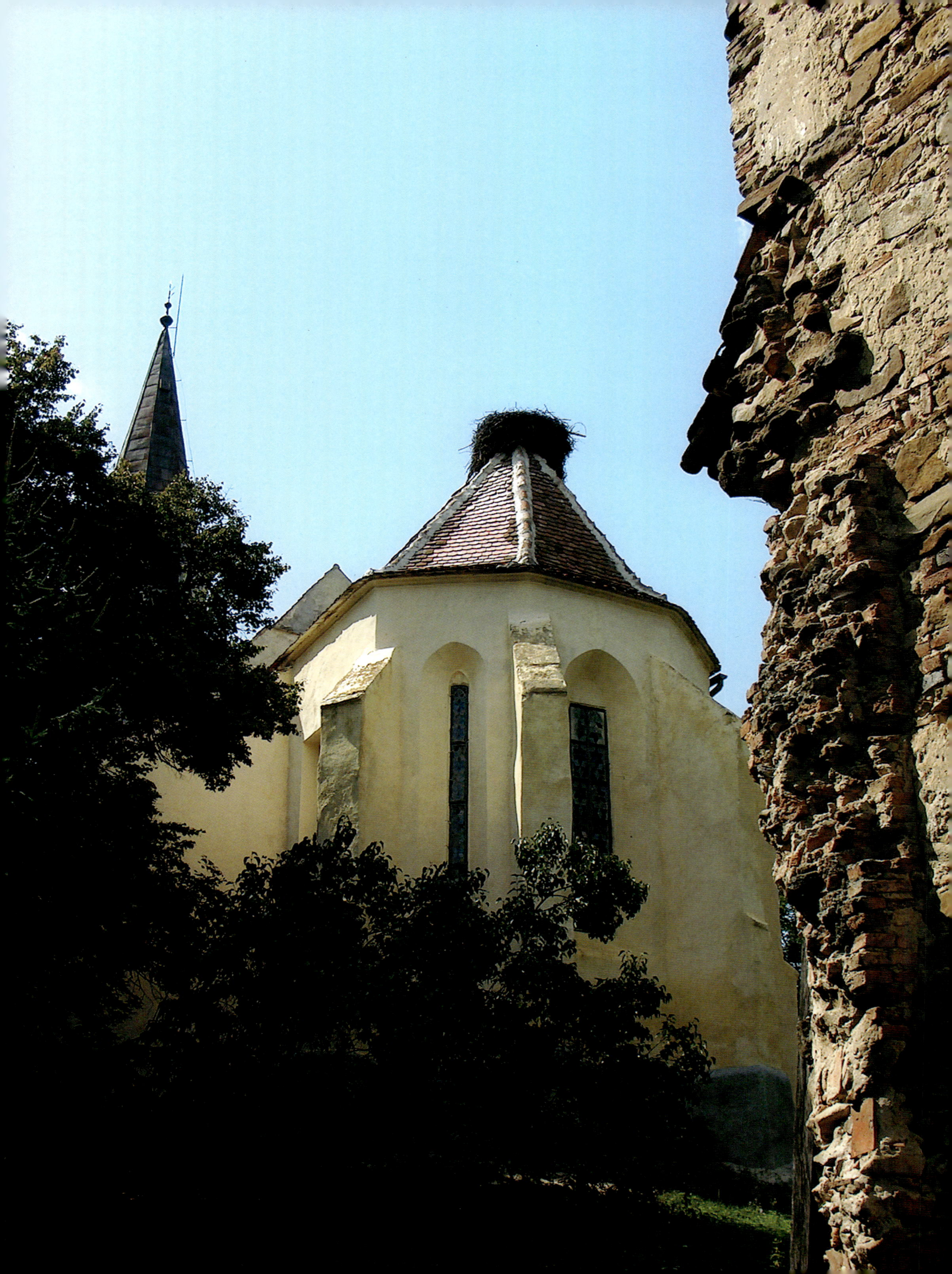

Alțâna
Alzen

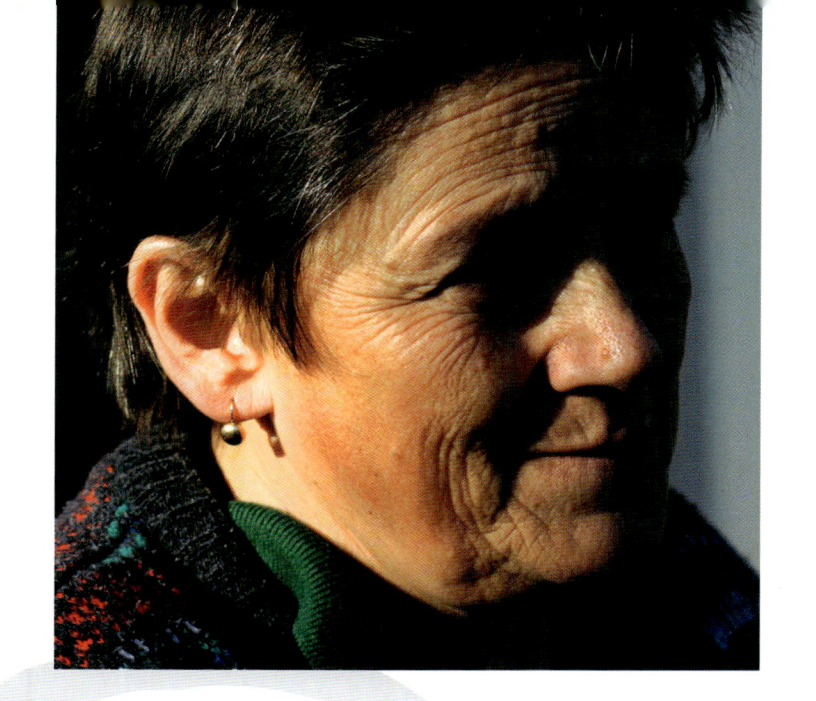

Hosman

Holzmengen

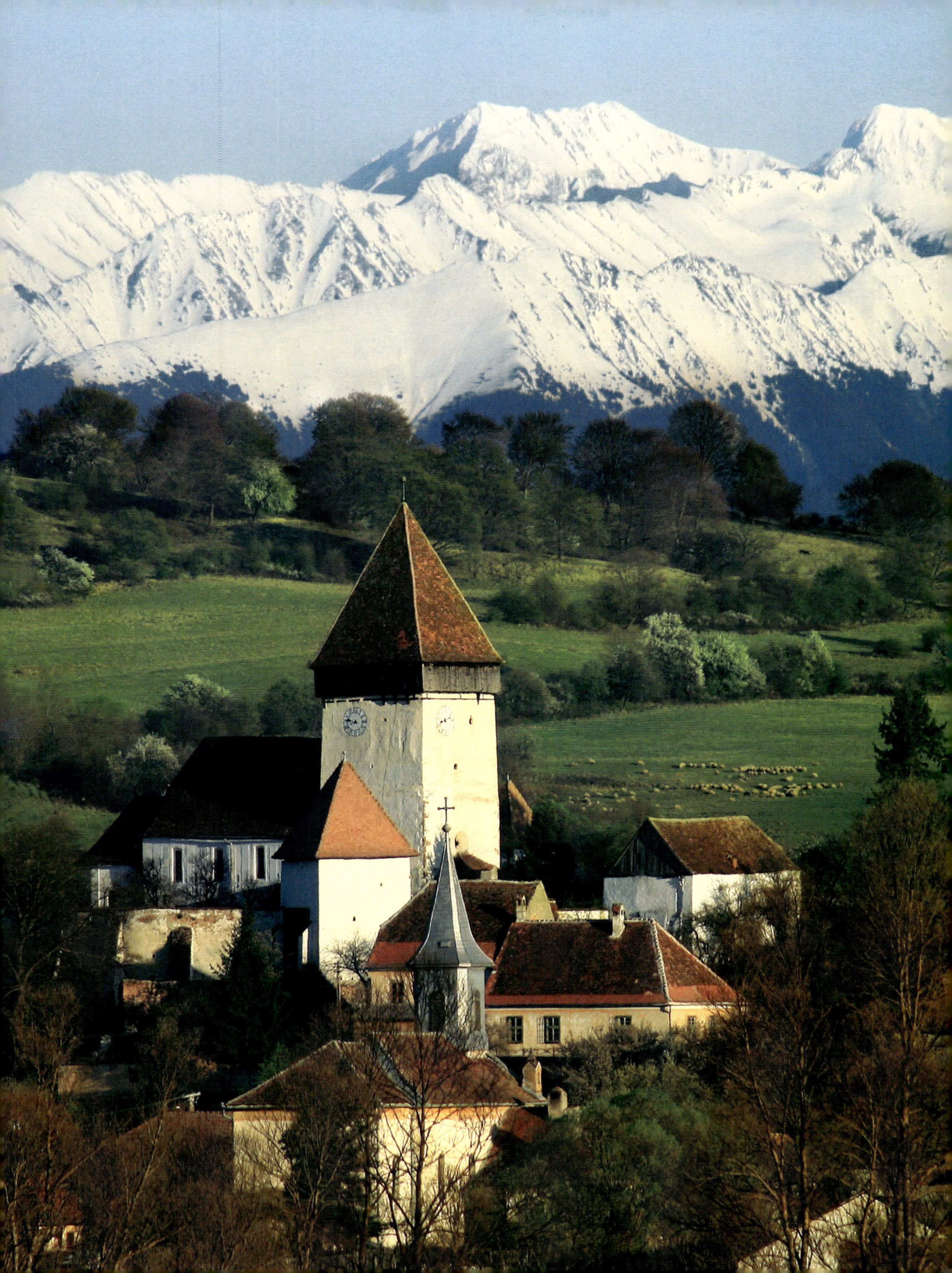

Slimnic
Stolzenburg

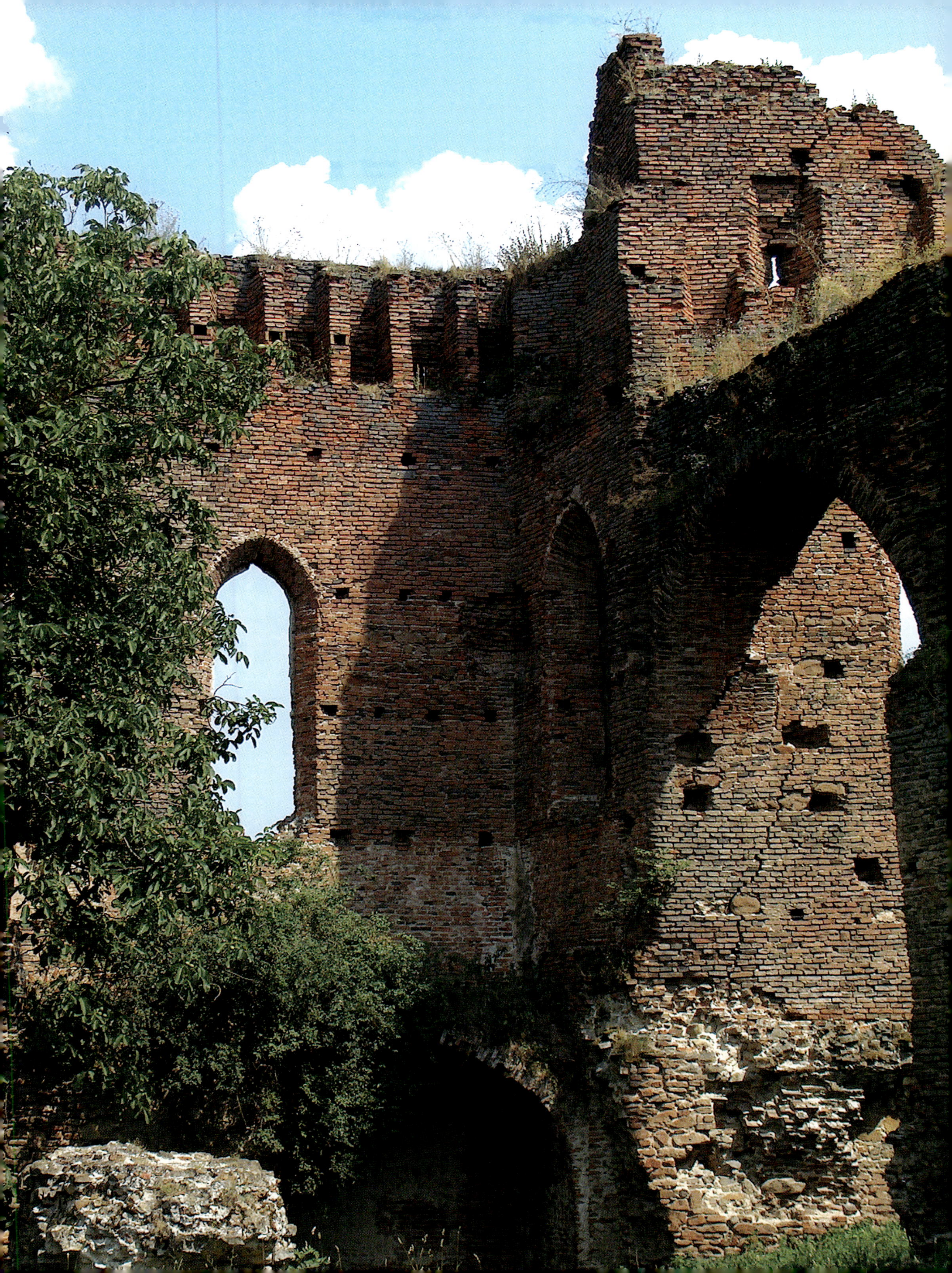

CISNĂDIE
HELTAU

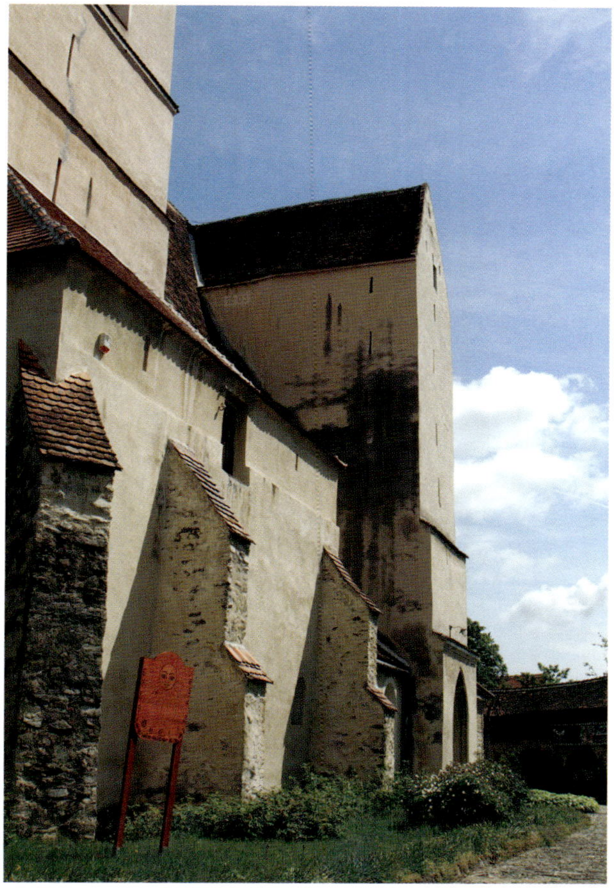
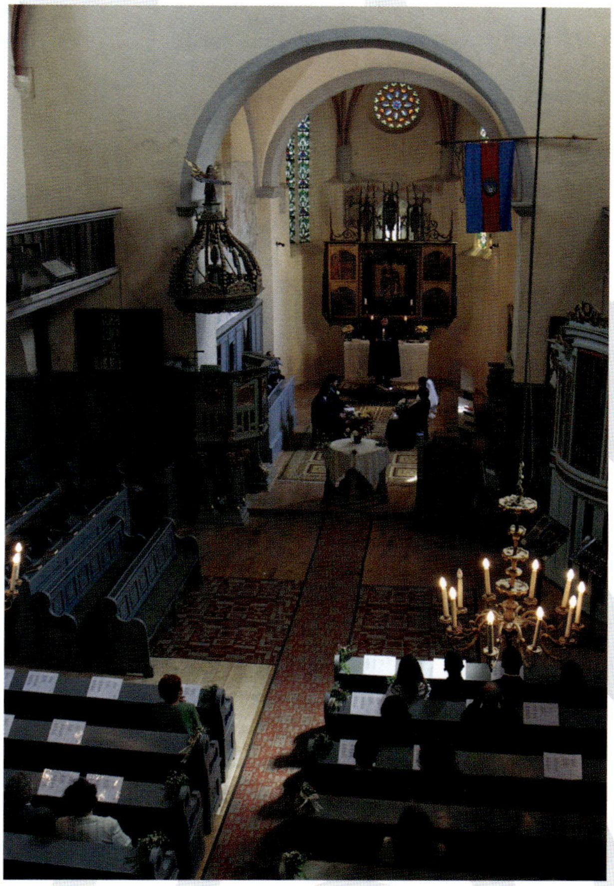
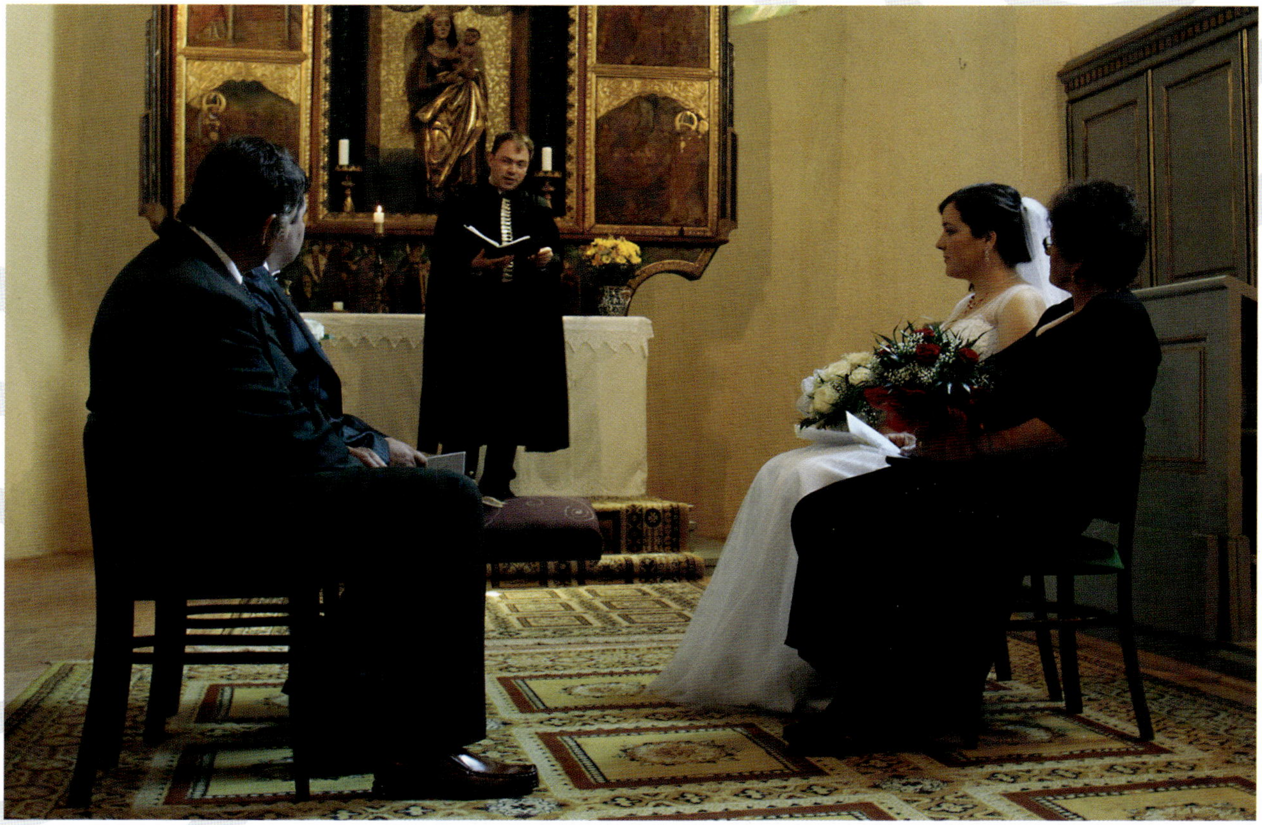

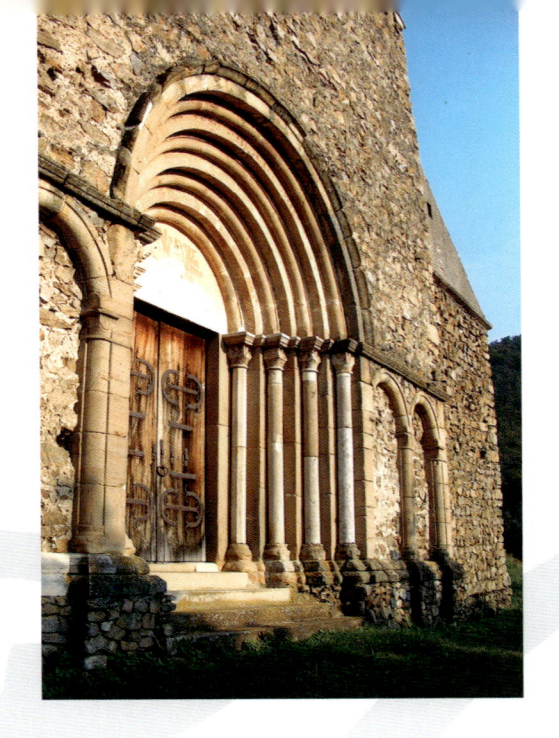

Cisnădioara

Michelsberg

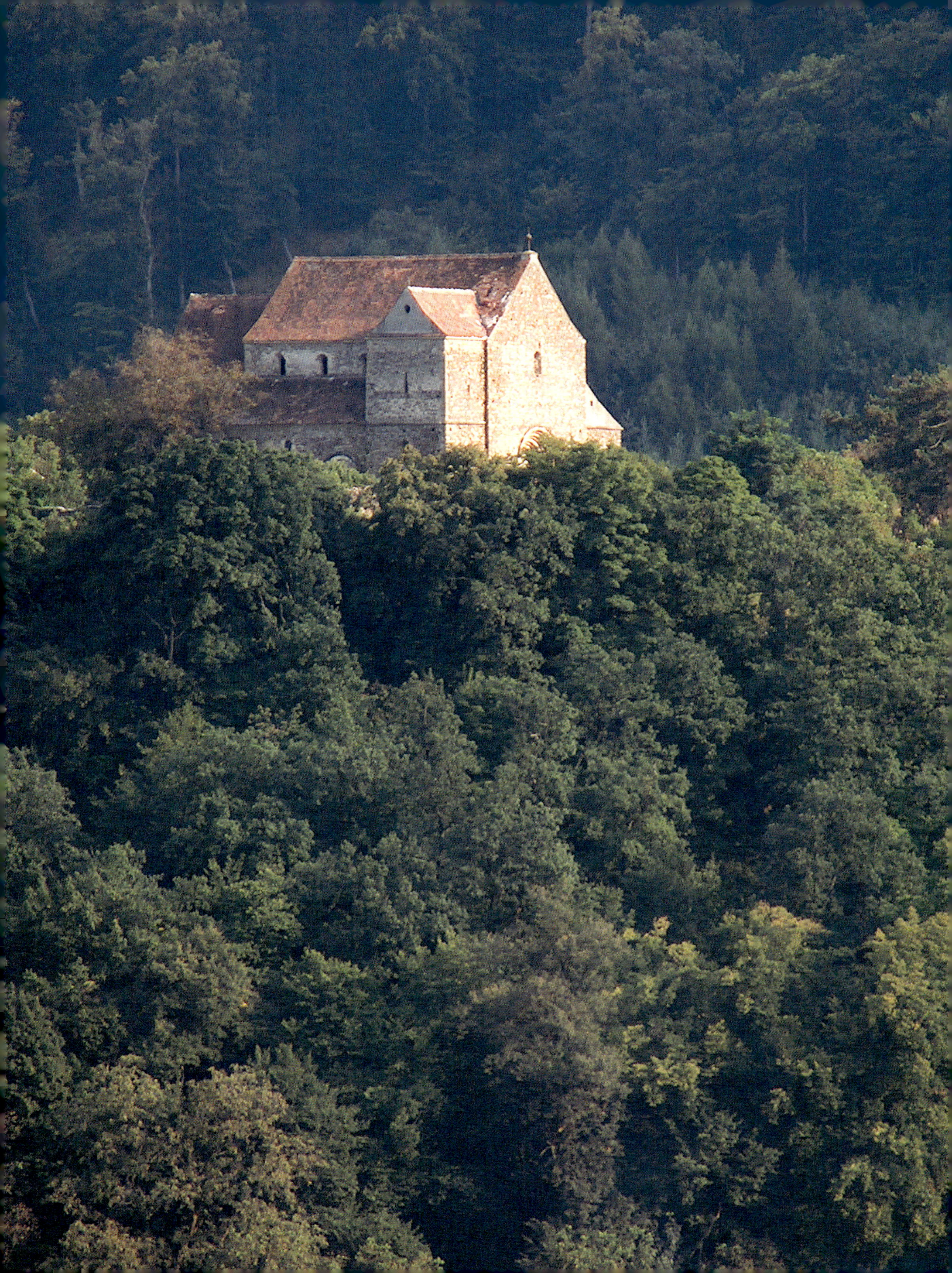

CÂLNIC
Kelling

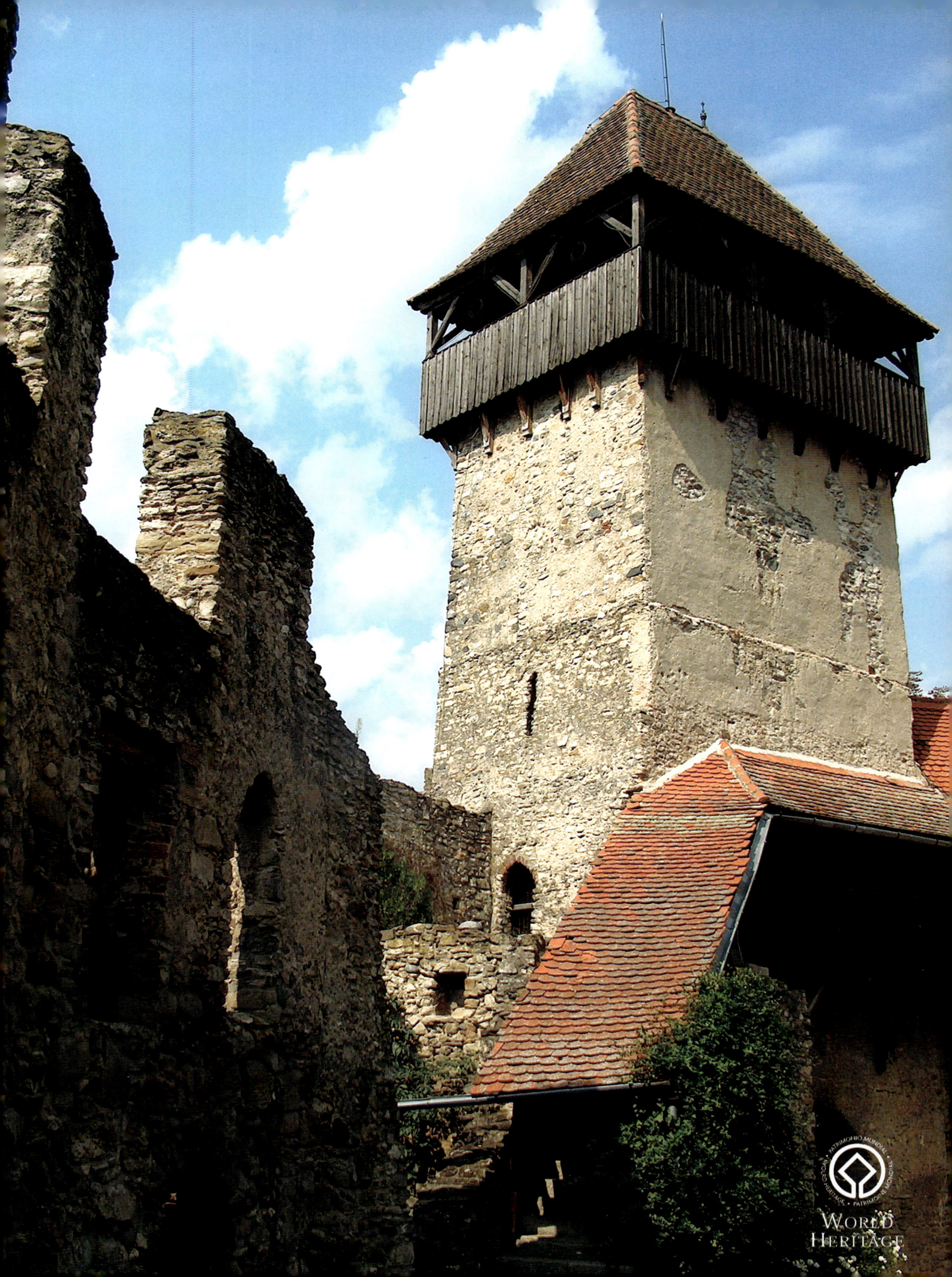
WORLD
HERITAGE

Sibiu

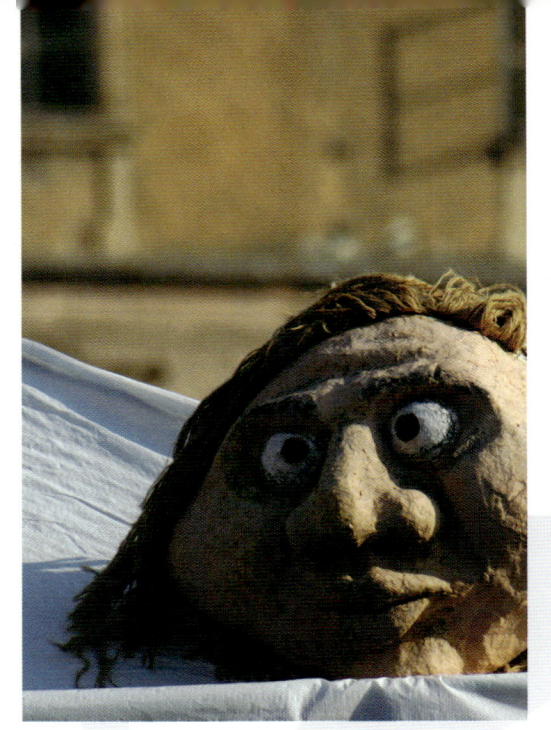

Hermannstadt

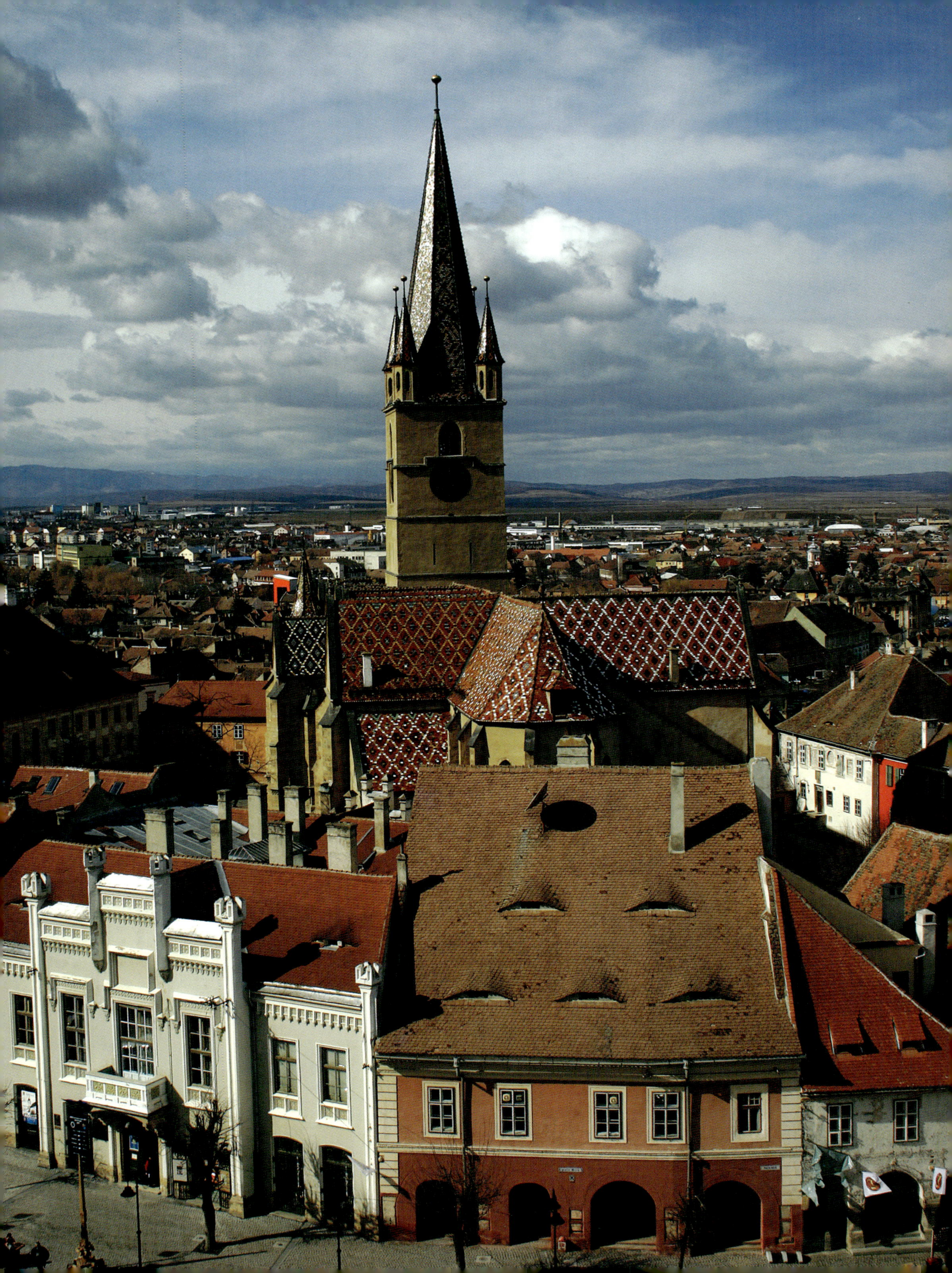

Foreword/Einleitung.................................5

Brașov ....8 - 33
    Râșnov (Rosenau)
    Brașov (Kronstadt)
    Hărman (Honigberg)
    Prejmer (Tartlau)
    Rotbav (Rothbach)
    Cața (Katzendorf)
    Drăușeni (Draas)
    Homorod (Hamruden)
    Bunești (Bodendorf)
    Viscri (Deutsch-Wißkirch)
    Meșendorf (Meschendorf)
    Criț (Deutschkreuz)

Sighișoara - Mediaș..........................34 - 87
    Saschiz (Keisd)
    Cloașterf (Klosdorf)
    Archita (Arkeden)
    Sighișoara (Schäßburg)
    Apold (Trappold)
    Daia (Denndorf)
    Daneș (Dunesdorf)
    Seleuș (Groß-Alisch)
    Laslea (Großlasseln)
    Mălâncrav (Malmkrog)
    Valchid (Waldhütten)
    Copșa Mare (Großkopisch)
    Biertan (Birthälm)
    Richiș (Reichesdorf)
    Alma Vii (Almen)
    Moșna (Meschen)
    Brăteiu (Pretai)
    Dârlos (Durles)
    Curciu (Kirtsch)
    Băgaciu (Bogeschdorf)
    Velț (Wölz)
    Bazna (Baaßen)
    Mediaș (Mediasch)
    Valea Viilor (Wurmloch)
    Ighișu Nou (Eibesdorf)
    Axente Sever (Frauendorf)

Agnita - Sibiu................................88 - 123
    Brădeni (Henndorf)
    Agnita (Agnetheln)
    Merghindeal (Mergeln)
    Dealu Frumos (Schönberg)
    Cincu (Großschenk)
    Seliștat (Seligstadt)
    Cincșor (Kleinschenk)
    Veseud (Zied)
    Chirpăr (Kirchberg)
    Cârța (Kerz)
    Alțâna (Alzen)
    Hosman (Holzmengen)
    Slimnic (Stolzenburg)
    Cisnădie (Heltau)
    Cisnădioara (Michelsberg)
    Câlnic (Kelling)
    Sibiu (Hermannstadt)

Acknowledgements

Many thanks to:

UNESCO Venice Office, European Institute of Cultural Routes, Râșnov Town Hall, The Romanian Group for an Alternative History, Mima Atelier, Truverii, Hosman Durabil, Wanderlust Tour, 764-211 Mocănița, Reky Travel

Hanna Derer, Matteo Rosati, Christa Richter, Cristian Sencovici, Manfred Kravatzky, Werner Hubatsch, Nicoleta Zagura, Bogdan Hrib, Radu Oltean, Alexandra Bardan, Claudia Câmpeanu, Sherry Huckabee, Peter Suciu, Eva Albert, Irina Secărescu

Credits:
Photos: Voichița Maican, Alexandru Purice, Iulian Cuțui, Irina Cristian, Mihai Dragomir, Nicolae Pepene, Daniel Secărescu
Legends: Laura Jiga Iliescu
Translators: Ilinca Maican, Christa Richter, Cristian Sencovici
Coordinator: Mihai Dragomir